WOMEN EMPOWERMENT IN GARHWAL HIMALAYAS

WOMEN EMPOWERMENT IN GARHWAL HIMALAYAS
Constraints and Prospects

Editors
Dr. (Mrs.) Annpurna Nautiyal
Dr. (Ms.) Himanshu Bourai

Assistant Editors
Dr. R.N. Gairola
Dr. M.M. Semwal

KALPAZ

Women Empowerment in Garhwal Himalayas : Constraints and Prospects

Rs. 750

ISBN: 978-81-7835-777-5

The views expressed in the papers are there of the authors themselves. The do not reflect the views of the editors
Published in 2009 in India by
Kalpaz Publications
C-30, Satyawati Nagar,
Delhi-110052
E-mail: kalpaz@hotmail.com
Phone : 9212729499

Laser Type Setting by: Rudra Computer Graphics, Delhi
Printed at : G. Print Process, Delhi

Contents

Preface

Women constitute nearly 50 percent of the total population in the country but their participation and representation in the political institutions is much less than their population. It cannot be considered a good omen for a democratic system as without the proper representation of the women it can neither function successfully nor can it be called fair and justified. Without equitable representation of the women such democracy would not be real but a crippled one. The World Congress of Beijing in 1995 reiterated the importance of increasing women's participation in all spheres of life. This is the first and most important step towards women empowerment as well as for strengthening the democratic process also. The degree and level of women's participation in socio-economic and political development programmes however, differs from country to country and even regions within a country, especially in a country like India where the regional variations regarding levels of development, urbanization and education are massive. In view of this actually women's participation needs to be studied and viewed in relation to their particular regional environment, socio-cultural and economic conditions and development. Ironically in India even after six decades of developmental efforts undertaken through the various plans and schemes by the governments and non-governmental and other organizations, the empowerment process of the rural people particularly the women in social, economic and political sphere has not taken place as desired. The lack of empowerment in real sense has been considered as a major threat and enigma to overall improvement of the life style of the people particularly women in the rural area. Unfortunately even after several years of efforts from all concerned the hopes, aspirations and dreams of rural people especially the women at large have not been fulfilled, hence there is an urgent need for integrated and holistic development based on equality, security, health and hygiene, complete fiscal, monetary and social well being of these targeted groups.

In the present book "Women Empowerment in Garhwal Himalayas: Constraints and Prospects" an attempt has been made to analyze the various problems and constraints confronting the women empowerment in the Gahwal Himalayas. Women in Uttarakhand due to looking after the domestic as well as the agriculture work are considered the backbone of the hill economy but from the view point of their empowerment and development their condition is not different from the other women of the country whereas their life style, living conditions and atmosphere is entirely different and difficult. Since Uttarakhand was created as the 27th state of the Indian union in November 2000 due to the pressures generated by a mass movement to demand a state based on the just, equitable and holistic development of the region therefore, the people hoped that their concerns for the continued deprivation and economic backwardness of the region would get proper attention in their own state. Interestingly women of this area though facing several hardships, crunch of time due to excessive workload and battling all the problems alone due to the male migration which is the result of the lack of industrial development or sources of employment, have participated in all the movements staged by the people for socio-political welfare and environmental protection. Be it the famous 'Anti-Liquor Movement of 1960's,

'Nsha Nahi Rojgar Do' Movement of the 1980 'Chipko Movement' of 1970s or the historic 'Uttarakhand State Movement' of the 1990's, the women have always played a significant role in all these issues of social concern. The spontaneous participation of the women in these movements on the one hand exhibits their anxiety towards the welfare of the society and awareness for the cause but on the other their activism also signifies their circumstantial compulsions, sensibilities and attempts to divert their energies from eco-social deprivation to eco-political activism. The present work also attempts to explore the possibilities of playing a more vital and dynamic role by the women of Garhwal Himalayas in regional as well as national development programmes.

This book mainly consists of the papers presented during the National Seminar organised by the department of political science to probe and discuss the issues of women empowerment its problems and prospects in the Garhwal Himalayas. The editors are especially thankful to the University Grants Commission, New Delhi for providing the financial support under its SAP-DRS Programme under which this seminar was organized. We also acknowledge our deep sense of gratitude to the authors who have contributed their papers based on primary data which forms the core of the research work. We would also like to convey our thanks to the faculty, staff and research scholars of the department of Political Science, HNB Garhwal University, for extending their kind co-operation.

Annpurna Nautiyal
Himanshu Bourai

Introduction

Annpurna Nautiyal and Himanshu Bourai

Women in India constitute half of the population but neither have they had easy access to power structure, nor are they able to overcome their age old inequality and subordination. Women's participation in development programmes, as a decision-maker and identity as a group is still not acceptable in the society. Actually since long the women have always remained in the periphery whether it is related to the processes of rural development or social transformation. Unfortunately this situation is prevailing despite the fact that participation of women in development programmes at all levels is considered as the most effective tool of removing their inequality and powerlessness. It is believed that the non inclusion of women in different bodies in accordance to their numbers and ineffective implementation and monitoring of the schemes and programmes designed for women's welfare even the Panchayati Raj institutions can fail in empowering the women in real sense of the term. If we talk in terms of women empowerment in the context of Uttarakhand we find that with the implementation of the 33 percent (presently 50 percent in Uttarakhand) reservation to the women in the local bodies under the provisions of the 73 rd and 74th amendment acts the women in a large number can be seen taking benefit of these provisions at the grass root level and also showing their caliber in the local bodies. However, the prevalence of the Pradhan Pati system even after the implementation of these provisions of empowerment not only makes a mockery of the clauses meant for the empowerment of the women but also indicates the poor status of the women in society. This also suggests that there is still a need to assess the reasons for such situation and device the ways and means to help the women to become empowered in the real sense of the term.

An assessment of the situation of the hill women of Uttarakhand, who have always taken active part in the movements like Chipko, Uttarakhand, Anti-Mining and Anti Liquor etc exhibits that they are still living in deprived conditions and their social, economic and political condition is also deplorable. It also shows that the problems, issues, needs and priorities of hill women tend to be different from the other regions and areas due to the tough geographical and socio-economic conditions. They have to earn their livelihood in difficult circumstances as on account of the non productivity of agriculture and absence of other job avenues, the migration of the male population to the plain areas for livelihood also forces the women to shoulder the responsibility of the agriculture besides the domestic work. The dual responsibility only adds to their miseries in the form of excessive work load without any monetary benefit. Importantly, in spite of hard efforts by women to sustain agriculture the food grain availability in the hills remains approximately for six months of the year only. In fact, the agricultural economy remains primitive and ecologically unsustainable. Past experiences reveal that the toil and hardship of rural women continues to be unabated in harsh surroundings and their work load has increased considerably over the years without much benefit trickling down either from the panchayats or state or rural development programmes. Due to over work the women neither get time to participate in any training or educative programmes meant for their development and awareness, nor they get any incentive for doing so. Therefore, in the absence of knowledge, interest and awareness about their rights and duties, the clauses of empowerment fail to make a major difference in the lives of a large number of women in hill areas. The dependence on the male members of the family for knowledge, awareness and execution of the responsibilities in some cases also creates problems and hampers the empowerment of the women.

Actually there are innumerable issues of the hill women, on which policy decision and concrete actions needs to be taken. In view of the above scenario and to explore the ways and means for evolving strategies for developing the leadership and entrepreneurial skills and involving women in large numbers in planning process a two days National Seminar on Women Empowerment in Garhwal Himalays: Constraints and Prospects' was organized by the department of Political Science, HNB Garhwal University, Srinagar, Garhwal in November 2007. Besides the above issues the participants of the seminar also deliberated on the effective instruments for bringing about social and economic changes to enable the women to fight the oppression and exploitation, gaining political rights in real sense and making effective contribution and representation in development programmes as well as Panchayati Raj system. The seminar was significant from the point of view that an attempt was also made to look at the lacunas of the present developmental programmes which claim to ensure full empowerment and representation of the women at the state as well as the national level. This book consists of some of the scholarly papers which were presented in this seminar. The papers thus compiled in this book have focused on the issues of women empowerment, women participation in developmental and environmental programmes and Panchayati Raj institutions in Uttarakhand, leadership capabilities among women in Uttarakhand, women's contribution towards Socio-Economic-Environmental issues, women's role as Activists in Uttarakhand etc.

The first paper of the book by P.C. Badola on "Women Empowerment Concept and Prospects" discusses the issue of women empowerment, its meaning and realities. As empowerment not only means equal representation in education, health and nutrition but also the economic independence, legal awareness and organizational support therefore he feels that education is an important variable of women's empowerment in Panchayati Raj Institutions. In view of this he has emphasized that the first and foremost step for empowering women representatives is the removal of illiteracy among them and at least the minimum education should be made obligatory for, both, male and female leaders. He has also advocated the need for comprehensive training programmes to improve the competence and capacities of the women by conducting training camps at local levels. He has also stressed the need for attitudinal changes among the male members in the families so that women could get a chance to take part in political activities. He feels that the positive and healthy atmosphere must be created in the society by removing social evils like purdah system, dowry system, caste-system and other feudal and orthodox traditions which are still present in the male dominated rural society. For improving the picture of women empowerment he has suggested that the courses should be designed to inculcate the feelings of equality and responsibility among girls from the tender age to enable them to participate in public affairs later on.

Jyoti Tiwari in her paper "Social and Economic Empowerment of Women in India" has emphasized that there are many laws to protect women and also for empowering them but real empowerment of women would be possible only if they are given proper access to health care, quality education at all levels, safety at work place as well as at home, social security and an environment, free from any kind of discrimination. She says that women's health and nutritional status is bound by social and cultural factors. And malnutrition is a serious health concern for the Indian women. By referring to various studies which indicate that women do not get adequate nutrition during pregnancy and lactation which accounts for nearly 25 percent of maternal deaths world wide, the author has stressed that women's health and nutrition is a very basic issue and there is an urgent need to evolve strategies to ensure that women of all strata get proper health care and nutrition. She has also emphasized the necessity of eradication of social evils like child marriages, child labour, purdah system; dowry system, which stands in the way of women's development and empowerment and advocated the access to education, health, nutrition, water and sanitation as the essential requirements for women empowerment.

Annpurna Nautiyal in her Paper entitled "Women Empowerment in Uttarakhand: Prospects and Challenges" has analyzed and evaluated the issue of empowerment and women's life in the hill areas of the Garhwal Himalayas. She has highlighted that in the rural and remote hill areas of Garhwal Himalayas women are still leading a very tough life not only due to the tough geographical conditions but also due to other various problems. For example, agriculture, which is the mainstay of the 80 percent people of Garhwal Himalayas is highly unproductive because of the small agricultural fields, fragmented and scattered land holdings, lack of irrigation facilities and prevalence of traditional methods and practices of crop. In the absence of other means of suitable employment in the remote areas, the out-migration of the male population for the search of employment becomes a necessary survival strategy. While discussing the political empowerment, representation and participation of women in Garhwal Himalaya she says that the scenario of women's political participation and activism at the grass root level has changed slightly with the implementation of the 33 percent reservation for the women in the local bodies and Panchayati Raj Institutions. A field based study has been used to substantiate the fact that the women are playing an important role in all the fields from domestic to agriculture, from social issues like anti- liquor agitations, environmental issues like Maite movement or Chipko movement to political movement like the Uttarakhand movement. But on the other hand it has also been emphasized that women do take interest in the issues related to the welfare or betterment of the society however their life is still full of hardships. Due to the geographical factors as well as economic and social considerations they have to work for long hours which limit their resources and access to information, communication and awareness. Moreover despite their education, the mindset and attitude of the society and its women segment has not changed much as they still have a tendency of belittling their contribution and always playing second fiddle. It is due to this reason that the concerns towards their developmental needs and requirements is still lacking. She says on the basis of this study that in the rural villages much has to be done to improve the status of women, to change their mind set, to reduce their drudgery, to increase their self confidence and capacities. She also mentions that though the Government has launched various schemes for the education and betterment of the women like free education for the girl child and Sarv Sikshsa Abhiyaan (Education for All) but in the absence of proper infrastructure, economic empowerment and proper information these remain futile because these rarely reach to the poorest among the women. The best strategies for improving women's condition and participation in rural development in the Garhwal Himalayas could be providing more attention and priority to education especially for the girl child, publicizing the schemes for rural development more seriously, bringing change in the mind set by improving general awareness, reducing the drudgery of the women, increasing their self confidence and capacities for getting benefit of the policies and developing a better pattern of connection, awareness and real empowerment.

Rama Maikhuri in her paper "Empowering Hill Women in Rural Development through Education and Awareness" has focused on the role of education and awareness for the empowerment of rural women of hill areas. She says that despite playing a very important role in nurturing the family and agriculture there is a general lack of appreciation of women's role and skills in managing and looking after the responsibilities of their own families. Due to such apathy they are ignored in the various capacity building and training programmes in rural development and decision making processes. Their perspectives, needs, knowledge and contribution are also overlooked. In order to empower women through education and awareness the author has stressed the need of dissemination of information about rural development programmes and activities being executed by the state/central governments and their departments to the rural women. She also feels that education needs to be encouraged as a means of empowering women from grass root level and awareness programmes for women should also incorporate capacity building and skill developmental activities for rural development, training for formal decision making processes, leadership and strategic planning, confidence building and role in decision-making in local level governance etc. She has also advocated the need to frame policies that support mainstream gender issues and acknowledge women's capacity in managing their families, their resources. Hill women also need to be involved in various programmes and activities necessary for improving their capacities and addressing the issues relevant to rural development and given equal opportunities to participate in decision making and selection of appropriate programmes/activities for rural development. She has also emphasized the need for giving proper recognition to hill women's roles and services. She also feels that the rural women also need to be made fully aware of the rural development programmes supported by central/state governments in the agriculture, irrigation and water management, social forestry, small scale village and cottage industries, rural housing, drinking water, rural road network, rural electrification and non-conventional energy sources, poverty alleviation, education, cultural activities, health family welfare and sanitation, women and child development, and Panchayati Raj, etc. for their effective participation in local governance.

An attempt has been made by Archana Shah and Mani Kant Shah in their paper 'Female Foeticide and Status of Girl Child: Awareness, Problems and Solutions" to discuss and draw attention to one of the most disturbing trends in our country of declining Child Sex Ratio. The paper also discusses the trends, causes and consequences of dwindling CSR with special reference to Uttarakhand. The authors have emphasized that all talk of women empowerment is meaningless unless something tangible is done to capture this trend. They have highlighted that the male-female sex-ratio in the child population (0 – 6 years) for Uttarakhand, does not give a good picture rather it indicates towards a dangerous situation as Uttarakhand ranks as the seventh member in the community of states reporting low CSR. The 2001 Census shows that there are only 908 female children for every 1000 male children in the age-group of 0 – 6 years in Uttarakhand. This simply means there are about 92 missing girls for every thousand boys. As already established, there has been a significant decline in CSR over a span of ten years in Uttarakhand. In view of the authors the declining sex ratio indicates that Uttarakhand has also become a member of the community of states which are guilty of committing sex-selective genocide. The authors feel that this is the high time to pay attention towards this trend and also to take corrective measures to arrest this decline by adopting measures to control female feticide all over India. As the continuous decline in the CSR would create social tensions when the eligible men will be unable to find women to marry. This would escalate crimes against women and lead to greater incidence of rape, sharing of women within and outside wedlock, abductions, and in general, a reduction in women's freedom and mobility. The authors feel that Uttarakhand's potential inclusion in the group of DEMARU Daughter Eliminating Male Aspiring Rage for Ultrasound (in short Daughter Killers) states is not a laudable achievement.

Himanshu Bourai in her paper "Women Participation in Watershed Management: A Field Study of Garhwal and Shiwalik Hills" discusses about women's participation in watershed management programmes. This study is basically a field based study which highlights that women are the most important component of any developmental schemes devised for village development therefore, any plan which ignores women's participation cannot be successfully implemented. She feels that unfortunately women's participation in various schemes is still lacking in ratio to their population. Since most rural women are directly dependent on their immediate environment and their own skills in using these for the daily necessities of life therefore, women, particularly living in the rural areas of Third World countries, play a major role in managing natural resources – soil, water, forest and energy. Their tasks in agriculture and animal husbandry as well as in the household make them the daily mangers of the living environment. They have a profound knowledge of the plants, animals and ecological process around them. As they depend on their immediate environment therefore, they also happen to be the principal victims of environmental degradation. The problems of the women and environmental degradation are very much interrelated as both suffer and are marginalized by existing developmental policies. The author on the basis of the field data feels that though women have never been involved directly as a 'target group' in watershed management programmes in general and soil and water conservation programme in particular, yet these programmes have changed the nature of the natural resources especially that of soil, water and vegetation. Watershed management has now become a widely accepted technology for resource management in totality and women's participation in WSM is an important component of people's participation in WSM. The results reported in this study which was conducted in the Sukhomajri WSM, Relmajra WSM Chandrbadni and Danda WSM and Fakot WSM cover the extent of women's participation in WSM who took part in the preparation and planning of natural resource management and watershed management, their satisfaction level about monetary and the environmental benefits, involvement in taking decisions on the rights of the watershed management, the level of confidence to work on other developmental activities etc. The patterns of women's participation in WSM and the reasons of their low participation have also been identified. The low participation of women is the result of competition for land, problems of land tenure, absence of legal entitlement of land, lack of time left after domestic and agriculture work, cultural taboos and lack of familiarity with forestry, institutional and organizational support and participatory nature of meetings, no invitation to participate in the meetings, non suitability of the time and location, women's inhibition, women's illiteracy and lack of knowledge. Various strategies have also been suggested by the author to enhance women's voices and participation in WSM.

Namrata Sharma and R. C. Sharma in their paper "Measuring Women Empowerment Using Qualitative Response and Quantitative Causal Models With Conjoint-Simulation

Techniques" have clearly mentioned that empowering women and improving their status are essential ingredients for realizing the full potential of the social, political and economic development of the entire society as well as for achieving the goal of sustainable development. For realizing this objective consistent and scientific measurement of women empowerment at different levels and regions is desirable. In their paper they have developed a model of Research Methodology for measuring women's empowerment. They feel that the results of the empirical models, i.e. qualitative response and quantitative regression are likely to be useful in figuring out some of the most crucial factors by the social planners for any policy initiatives for improving the status and empowerment of women in the selected area of research. They also feel that these models are also very useful in generalizing the future research in this area. According to them the logit model and quantitative regression are powerful and scientific methods for analyzing the women empowerment. The conjoint-simulation analysis for both the models is proposed methodological innovations in this area of research.

Sunita Badola in her paper "Empowerment of Women with Reference to Women of Rural Uttarakhand" has basically discussed and analyzed the governmental policies after independence. She like many other authors also shares the view point that polity has undertaken various initiatives towards improving the socio-economic conditions of women and accentuating their participation in the social, economic, cultural and educational sectors. But, due to the short lived impact of these policies the condition and status of women remains unchanged. She has also highlighted that the introduction of Panchayati Raj has brought women to seats of power as village heads and at the block level, but on account of the want of training and experience in such matters, their position remains weak and their work is undertaken by their husbands who act as the Pradnans-Pati. In such conditions the political scene is once again dominated by men. In order to overcome the constraints she has stressed the need of providing proper education to the women. She has also advocated the need of providing some relief to the women from domestic duties so that they have time to use their potential in a better way as without these changes women empowerment cannot be achieved only through policy intervention.

Annpurna Nautiyal and Rakesh Negi in their paper on " Supporting Factors for Women's Participation and Success in Politics in Uttarakhand" say that though the women of Uttarakhand have been oppressed, under estimated and marginalized in the male dominated society however, during the last few decades, their personal, social, economic and cultural life has witnessed some transformation. With the improvement in women's educational standard both in rural and urban areas they are also showing an interest in participation in political, social, cultural and other activities. The reservation for women in the Panchayati Raj Institutions besides allowing their entry in to politics in a large number has also generated an interest towards the political activities. Their political participation and direct association with politics have opened new vistas for them. The findings and observations of this paper are based on the field data collected during the study. The authors have highlighted the fact that women from common background are still far away from the doorstep of politics and they are not seen anywhere in the race of political power sharing. Although women's participation has increased at the grass root level after the implementation of the 33 percent reservation and women have been able to capture non reserved seats also but barring a few the majority of the women are still dependent on their husbands or male members in performing their duties due to their illiteracy, inferiority complex, lack of self confidence and quality education etc. In view of this the authors feel that there is a need to change the scenario and create such opportunities and conditions which make women's entry in to politics easy and smooth and they are also able to leave their mark by actively working for the development of their area. Women's sincerity, integrity, judgment about the needs, priorities and commitment towards duty makes them a perfect candidate for bringing changes in political scenario which is full of corruption, deceit and non accountability. In view of this they feel that it is more than essential to ensure women's entry in to politics by providing them good quality education, grooming them for discharging their duties efficiently as well as reserving seats for them in parliament and assemblies also.

Anjali Bahuguna and M.M. Semwal in their paper "Empowerment of Women: A Case Study of District Uttarkashi In Uttarakhand" underline the fact that empowerment of women is a dynamic multidimensional process, which enables women to realize their full distinctiveness and powers in all spheres of life. Empowerment strategies consist of greater access to knowledge and resources, greater autonomy in decision making and greater ability to plan their lives, literacy and higher education, better health care for herself and her children, necessary financial and service support for self employment, opportunities for higher positions of power including governance and complete knowledge of her rights. They have mentioned that the process of empowering women in Uttarakhand specially in remote rural villages could be achieved only through a better approach for action through: creating a positive environment, eliminating discrimination against women and the girl child, ensuring access to health care, quality education at all levels, career and vocational guidance, employment and equal remuneration, strengthening legal system, changing societal attitudes and mindset for eliminating discrimination against women and providing equal access to participation and decision making for women in social, political and economic life of the nation. The authors hope that the Eleventh Five Year Plan will not only strengthen but also speed up the ongoing process and efforts of empowering women. The authors also feel that the Uttarakhand Government's decision to give fifty percent reservation to women candidates in Panchayati Raj Institutions in Uttarakhand is an important step for empowerment of women.

R.N. Gairola in his paper "Impact of Education on Women Empowerment in Uttarakhand" has discussed the role of education in women empowerment. According to him education is one of the most important factors which have a bearing on the thought patterns, personality structure, responsibility, obligations and empowerment. The movements for improving women's status all over the world have emphasized the value of education as an instrument for elimination of discrimination on grounds of sex. It is believed that education will bring about a reduction in the inequalities between sexes as well as improve and uplift women's subjugated position in the society. The author says that as education helps women to take independent decisions or make choices from the alternatives available therefore, the educational status or literacy of the women in any society is closely related to their empowerment, progress and development. His data based study clearly mentions that the prevalence of gender gap and disparity in literacy in Uttarakhand is the result of the lack of proper schooling facilities for the girls, lack of importance to female literacy, domestic and agricultural workload of the females etc. The author suggests that it is necessary to pay special attention to female education so that the gender gap in female literacy could be reduced. He feels that the spread of education among girls will help inculcate values, attitudes and orientations leading to socialization of women especially women of rural areas as well as their real empowerment. The strategy to achieve this goal according to the author is to provide meaningful and relevant education which should reflect the overall needs of the society and fulfill the diverse need of the society. In his view only such kind of education can become a potent instrument of women empowerment in Uttarakhand

In her paper "A Reflection on the Moral strategies to Address Gender Biasness" Indoo Pandey Khanduri highlights that the gender biasness in approach, attitude and thinking strategies is the greatest obstruction in the way of women's empowerment. She feels that the attempts for women empowerment and gender biasness are related in a piquant way, as both require a radical change in the distorted attitude and the attitude change of humans requires moral strategies and commitment to be followed at the ground level. Her paper attempts to explore the ways and means and moral strategies to reduce the gender biased approach, attitude and thinking and promotion of women empowerment in real sense of the term. In the first part of the paper the author has analyzed the meaning of gender biasness as well as the methods to search the root causes of gender biasness. She says that these could be searched in the very social structure, religious scriptures and even theoretical attempts in explaining human behavior in general and personality traits in particular. In the second part of this paper, the author has explained how gender biasness is damaging the women's rights and empowerment in terms of opportunity to take birth, upbringing, grooming their personality and potentiality. In the third and concluding part of this paper, the author has examined how the strategies of RAP group theory, egalitarian and liberation ethics are addressing the gender biasness for the cause of women empowerment and the real needs at ground level.

In view of the importance of the issue and the contribution of the women of the Garhwal Himalayas towards the social, economic and environmental welfare of the society, it is hoped that that this volume would be useful for the people who have an interest in the issues of hill development as well as for the policy makers, professionals, academicians and students to assess the constraints and the prospects of women empowerment.

Anil Dutta Mishra in his paper, "Empowerment through Political Participation" has mentioned very clearly that political participation of women is very essential for women empowerment. He says that Participation enables women to understand their own dignity and value. Women participation has three roles: educative, integrative and empowering. Women constitute half of the society and belong to all classes and all sections. So, the women's empowerment is not the question of one section only. It is ultimately the question of the entire society. It is an integral part of the entire social phenomenon. Human society cannot move forward without stirring half of its body, the women. Thus, it is in the social and national interest to draw womenfolk into the social and political process. Today women are connected directly or indirectly to the operation of society at every level, and at the same time occupy the aggregate position of outsiders. No one can deny the fact that for women's empowerment, their participation at every level and in every field is essential. The political space belongs to all citizens; politics is everyone's business and affects the lives of each of us... the more women are associated, in numbers corresponding to their percentage of the population, in the political decision making process, in parties, in elected bodies, in government and in international bodies, the more they can be associated with this process as protagonists the more they can change the modalities and outcomes of politics. In such situation only the concept of democracy would find concrete and tangible expression because democracy and the participation of women go hand in hand and promote each other mutually. He has also mentioned the major obstacles for women's participation in active politics. He says that the participation of women is influenced by the inter-related factors like the social status of women, their economic position, the cultural norms, and above all the regional outlook towards women's participation in the society. Access to significant decision-making position in the political parties continues to elude women. Women in the political world face peculiar problems which are totally unknown to their male counterparts. These inhibit their performance in the legislative and party work not only in India but also in the so-called emancipated societies of the developed countries. A variety of reasons account for women's diminished role in the political arena. These include tradition, physiology, lack of vertical mobility, concern for home and family, psychology and lack of patronage, particularly, from senior women politicians. In other words, political participation of women is severely limited due to a nexus of traditional factors like domination of Indian politics by patriarchal forces and the consideration of caste, class, religion, feudal and family status etc., all of these are parochial and favour men more than women. Consequently, women are still left on the periphery of the political process, and their political participation remains basically confined to elections. At the same time, there are several other socio-economic constraints which marginalize the women. Due to this the number of women in leadership positions at the local, village, district and national level is still not commensurate with their numbers in society. A woman in public life at the different level is as much part of the Indian Society as the woman who is confined to her home and family. Styles of functioning of such women in the three tier system of Panchayati Raj, or State Assemblies or Parliament are bound to be shaped by the cultural mosaic which is studded with the prescriptive and descriptive elements, codes of conduct, role models, political goals, values and ideals in transitions.

To increase women's participation in politics he has given some important suggestions like developing a long term process for bringing fundamental changes in all cultural, social, political and economic norms. Developing an entirely new way of thinking-in which the stereotyping of women and men no longer limits their choices, but gives way to a new philosophy that regards all people as essential agents of change and views development as a process of enlarging the choice of both sexes, not just one. Stages of emancipation of women, in any given country, lie in the mind of man and in the attitudes of their leadership and these two factors have mostly favored women in India. Besides this training is one of the most important mechanisms for improving women's participation in politics particularly for increasing women's access to the higher levels in national decision making bodies. He has also suggested that while training can be directed to improving women's skills in specific areas, particularly in management, gender sensitivity training needs to be given to both men and women to build awareness for removing the attitudinal barriers to women's participation, advancement and empowerment.

Pushpa Motiyani in her paper entitled "Culture of Peace through Strengthening Women's and Minority's Rights" clearly mentions that in the last forty years, the benefits of development have not reached to the poor of the developing countries adequately. The main reason behind this is the fact that, there are political, social and economic inequalities between and within nations. Ultimately, these inequalities lead to serious power differences, as a result of which the benefits of development are reaped only by the ruling classes. Unless we solve the developmental problems of these depressed masses of the developing countries, we cannot think of a just world order, based on human rights and peace. She has also discussed the culture of peace and human rights and mentioned that without peace we cannot achieve the goal of just and equal society. For this she has also highlighted the Gandhian view that the Human being is the supreme consideration and rights are inherent in human beings, irrespective of religion, race, colour, nationality, etc and peace is the prerequisite for all. Meeting the basic needs and welfare of all is embedded in Sarvodaya. The entire realm of Gandhian thought and action was to liberate man from the clutches of domination, exploitation and violence. Throughout his life, Gandhiji maintained and worked for the equality of woman with man. He believed in woman's ability, strength, will and character to stand on her own and to work with man. Gandhiji, had awakened the women folk, and made them to fight for their rights and freedom. He brought them into political arena from their home and convinced them to take active part in the Indian freedom struggle. Gandhiji believed that the secret of achieving world peace is equally in the hands of women and men. To attain peace in every walk of life a cumulative effort of both men and women backed by nonviolence, justice and equality is essential. While concluding her paper she has stressed that Gandhiji can be called a peace-maker because he worked earnestly for social justice and welfare of all. He also gave importance to fulfilling the basic human rights which are the components of peace. Therefore, in today's world, if we want to establish a civilization of peace and nonviolence, there is a need to give more importance to attainment of human rights of women, and weaker sections. Then only justice will come in the society and violence, discrimination, injustice towards women and weaker sections would be abolished which will lead the world towards a culture of peace. Gandhiji believed that the secret of achieving world peace is equally in the hands of women and men. To attain peace in every walk of life a cumulative effort of both men and women backed by nonviolence, justice and equality is essential.

List of Contributors

Dr. P.C. Badola
Head, Deptt. of Pol. Science Maharaj Singh College
Saharanpur-24 700 1

Dr. Jyoti Tiwari
Sr. Lecturer and Head Department of Home Science
H.N.B.Garhwal University
Srinagar (Garhwal), Uttarakhand

Dr. Annpuma Nautiyal
Professor and Head Department of Political Science
HNB Garhwal University, Srinagar, Garhwal,
Uttarakhand, 246174, India

Dr. Rama Maikhuri,
Reader, Department of Education, HNB Garhwal University,
Srinagar, Garhwal-246174 Uttrakhand

Mrs. Archana Shah
Lecturer, Department of Home Science HNB Garhwal
University
SRT Campus, Badhshahi Thaul
Uttarakhand

Dr. Mani Kant Shah
Department of Sociology HNB Garhwal University
SRT Campus, Badhshahi Thaul
Uttarakhand

Dr. Himanshu Bourai
Professor, Department of Political Science HNB Garhwal University
Srinagar-246174 , Uttarakhand

Dr. Namrata Sharma
Reader- Academic Staff College Devi Ahilya University-Indore

Dr. R C Sharma
Professor-School of Future Studies and Planning
Devi Ahilya University-Indore

Dr. Sunita Badola
Reader, Department Education HNB Garhwal University Srinagar (Garhwal) Uttarakhand-246174,

Mr. Rakesh Negi
Project Fellow UGC-SAP-DRS Programme Department of Political Science
HNB Garhwal University Srinagar-246174 , Uttarakhand

Dr. Anjali Bahuguna
Professor, Department of Economics HNB Garhwal University
Srinagar-246174 , Uttarakhand

Dr. M.M. Semwal
Professor Department of Political Science HNB Garhwal University Srinagar-246174 , Uttarakhand

Dr. R.N. Gairola
Professor, Department of Political Science HNB Garhwal University Srinagar-246174 , Uttarakhand

Dr. Indoo Pandey Khanduri
Reader, Department of Philosophy, HNB Garhwal University, Srinagar (Garhwal) Uttarakhand-246174 INDIA, Email-indookhanduri@rediffmail.com

Dr. Anil Dutta Mishra
Depl1ty Director National Gandhi Museum Rajghat, New Delhi

Dr. Pushpa Motiyani
Reader and Head
Department of Gandhian Studies Peace Research center Gujarat Vidyapith
Ahmedabad-380014

Dr.Bhuwan Chandra Upreti
Professor and DirectorSouth Asia Studies Center University of Rajasthan Jaipur (Rajasthan)

Women Empowerment Concept and Prospects

P.C. Badola

India's first Prime Minister Pandit Jawahar Lal Nehru believed that "The status of women indicates the character of the country" in fact the social standing of any society is determined by the social status of its women. As women have played a key role in the evolution of mankind therefore the society's status rises and falls with the status of the women. Social structure, cultural norms and the value system are important determinants of women's roles and their status in the society (Pujari and Kausik, 1994). It is a well recognized fact since the ancient times that the mother is the first and the best teacher a person can have. The status of women in the society depends on the role played by them and how others look at their role. Intellectually, mentally and spiritually a woman is equivalent to a men and she can participate in every activity with equal competence as a man. However, everywhere in the world women are accorded a lower status than men. Describing the status of women all over the world, Gustave Speth in his Foreword to *Human*

Development Report, 1995 wrote that, "Women still constitute 70 per cent of the world's poor, and 2/3rds of the world's total illiterate. They occupy 14 per cent of managerial and administrative jobs, 10 per cent of parliamentary seats and 6 per cent of Cabinet positions. In many legal systems they are still unequal. They often work longer hours than men but much of their work remains unvalued, unrecognized and unappreciated, and the threat of violence stalks their lives from cradle to grave."

Women's Condition and Rights: Brief Historical Background

In India, too, during the *Vedic* period the daughter was not as welcome as the son. In *Atharvaveda* there are examples of rituals to ensure that the birth of a son was preferred than a daughter (III; 23; 4, 2) however the birth of the daughter was not a source of consternation to the family in the *Vedic* ages. In the *Upanisads* one finds mention of certain rituals recommended for ensuring the birth of a scholarly daughter. The position of women was, however, not the same throughout the *Vedic* period. During the later *Vedic* period, her position deteriorated because of a gradual decline in female education as religious rights of the average woman were curtailed. It was during the Brahmanic period, when Manu gave the code of conduct for women which ensured their subordination and imposed several restrictions on them. In the age of Jainism and Buddhism some improvement in the status of women was observed. In the *Jataka* books of Buddhists, however, women were defined as thieves, unreliable and wild. The concept that woman is inferior to man came to be universally accepted by people in medieval times. While the *Vedic* period is considered as the golden age of women, the period of Muslim rule is considered to be the dark age by the historians. The customs of *Sati*, child marriage, and restrictions on Widow Marriage were the factors responsible for injustice to women. The position of women in the beginning of 19th century was, indeed, very deplorable. Various socio-religious reform movements were started for the salvation of women. The wave of reform in the 19th century was initiated by Raja Ram Mohan Roy and followed up by Ishwar Chandra Vidyasagar, Dayananda Saraswati, Kesav Chandra Sen, Mahadev Govind Ranade, etc. Yet their position did not improve satisfactorily. In the 20th century, a series of steps were taken to create awareness and providing equal opportunities to them. Notable ladies like Mrs. Annie Besant, Mrs. Sarojini Naidu, Durgabhai Deshmukh, Kasturba Gandhi and Sister Nivedita became prominent in this sphere. The Sati Prevention Act, 1829 prohibited the custom of burning a Hindu widow alive in the funeral pyre of her husband. But, unfortunately, the practice is still in vogue among some orthodox Hindus. To put an end to this crime, the Sati Prevention Act was passed by the Government of India in 1987. During the British Rule itself, the Child Marriage Restraint Act was passed in 1929 to prevent the early marriage of girls in their tender age, but the system of child marriage still persists in India.

After independence women were given equal rights to participate in the social, economic, political and developmental policies by the constitution. Women are entitled to vote in elections, eligible for election to all publicly elected bodies, and to hold public office and exercise all public functions on equal terms with men. Article 38 of the Constitution provides for the welfare of women in matters relating to social, political and economic justice. Article 39 provides the citizens, men and women equal right to an adequate means of livelihood. It also provides for equal pay for equal work for, both genders. The most remarkable Act welcomed by the people of India was the Dowry Prohibition Act of 1961. This Act prohibits giving dowry in any form. This practice is considered a social evil and a burning problem in our society. As dowry deaths and problems connected with dowry are increasing day by day, the Government of India felt the need for amending the Criminal law in 1986. As such, an amendment was made in Section 304-B of IPC by the Act 43 of 1986.

Women were also given the property rights and the property of women was divided in to two heads (a) *stridhan*, and (b) women's estate. *Stridhan* includes, mainly, movable property such as ornaments, jewellery, dresses, gifts and bequests from relatives, gift and bequests from strangers, property acquired by self-exertion and mechanical arts, property purchased with *stridhan*, acquired by compromise, by adverse possession, obtained in lieu of maintenance and inheritance, and share obtained on partition enumerate women's property. Dowry and traditional presents made to a wife at the time of the marriage constitutes her *stridhan*, and if the husband or her in-laws refuse to give it back to her, on demand, they would be considered guilty of criminal breach of trust. The Hindu Women's Right to Property Act, 1937 which has been repealed by the Hindu Succession Act 1956, also recognized the widow's right to property. For instance, if a Hindu dies leaving behind his separate property, his own widow, son's widow and grandson's widow, each will take one-third share in the property.

The Hindu Marriage Act of 1995, brought, for the first time, the right of divorce to women-folk. Prior to this, normally a Hindu woman could not even imagine of divorce from her husband. The right of widow remarriage is also provided in this Act. Though there was already an act called the Hindu Widow Remarriage Act (1856) but this could not stop the social humiliation faced by the Hindu widows. Any woman victim of immoral traffic can seek justice in court against the offender under the Immoral Traffic (Prevention) Act 1956 and also by the Act 44 of 1986. Further, to protect the women and their dignity, Indecent Representation of Women (Prohibition) Act was passed in 1986. Indian Constitution also provides special consideration for certain category of citizens, which is reflected in the laws regarding Muslims. A Muslim divorcee is entitled to claim maintenance only for *Iddat* period —three months after pronouncing *Talaque*. This right is provided under Muslim Women Protection of Rights on Divorce Act of 1986.

The constitutional provision of respecting 'personal law' of various communities has resulted in perpetuating unequal status of women in various religious communities. The personal laws of Hindus, Muslims, Parsis etc., directly affect women's lives and status. These laws are not only discriminatory but they also have a deep rooted prejudice against women. None of them considers women as independent human being with individuality, but as dependent on father, husband or son. Although there is no denying the fact that throughout the ages parents have loved their daughters as much, and sometimes even more, than their sons but, ironically, reaction to the birth of a girl child in Indian Society is generally a mixture of tenderness as also sadness as the parents always desire a son due to the ingrained preference for sons in the Indian psyche. The declining Sex Ratio in India (Table 1) could be a reflection of the son preference in the country:

Table 1 : Trend of Sex Ratio in India (1911-2001)

Year	*Population (in millions)*	*Sex ratio (female per 1000 males)*
1911	252.1	972
1921	251.3	964
1931	279.0	955
1941	318.7	950
1951	361.1	945
1961	439.2	946
1971	548.2	941
1981	683.3	930
1991	846.3	927
2001	1027.0	933

Source : Census Reports.

Women's participation and representation in political activities and public life has also been very marginal, although they make up approximately 50 per cent of world's population. Their representation in Parliament has just increased from 4.4 per cent to 8.3 per cent over a period of about 50 years:

Table 2 : Women's Participation in Parliament (in per cent)

Year	*Lok Sabha*	*Rajya Sabha*
1952	4.4	7.3
1962	6.7	7.6
1971	4.2	7.0
1980	7.9	9.8
1991	7.16	15.5
1996	7.18	8.63
1998	7.5	...
1999	8.6	...
2004	8.3	...

Source : Election Commission, Government of India.

Empowerment of Women

Empowerment implies a state of mind and attitude of a person. Empowerment emerges in the form of awareness in women, enables them to face challenges boldly, and overcome barriers in their life. They increase their ability to shape their own lives and environment through empowerment. Empowerment is a process which strengthens the competence of people, in general, and the oppressed sections, in particular. Empowerment is used for ensuring social transformation and economic development of a society as well as giving power to certain underprivileged sections of society. It also includes political participation and acquiring the capabilities to influence the political decisions effectively. Development is synonymous to participation which can be encouraged by the empowerment of alienated sections of society. Participation means sharing or taking part or involvement in the development process or role in decision making. It can be interpreted as empowering the weaker sections of society to take independent, collective and voluntary action in order to enhance their living standard and social status. Thus, the concept of empowerment has become essential and acceptable addition to the process of development and it has started to influence the democratic discourse and development strategies of a state. It requires full participation of the people in formulation, execution and evaluation of decisions, determining the functions, and the well being of our society. The strengthening of capacities is the main objective of development process and it can be achieved through empowerment of the alienated sections, to enable them to help themselves and to manage their own affairs in the society. The betterment of these sections can be expected only by their acquiring competence and creating adequate capacities to enable them to participate actively in socio-economic and political affairs of the state. The underprivileged groups like women, dalits, tribals, peasants and labourers have been engaged in the struggle for power, and these groups can be empowered by ensuring their participation in the development process. Actually for the progress and prosperity of India, the progress of women and the other marginalized groups is essential. The role of women can be summed up in 4 M's — Match, Mother, Manager and Mover.

In the context of the women empowerment means the equal representation in the following:

- Education
- Health and Nutrition
- Economic Independence
- Legal Awareness
- Organizational support, and
- Intervention Programmes.

In the last two decades women have been demanding a legitimate autonomy in all matters that have a bearing on their empowerment. A number of women's movements took place in India after 1975 to create awareness in the minds of all. The International Women's Year (1975) spearheaded the movement for equality of men and women, and the integration of women in the development process for strengthening the world peace. The Decade of Women (1975-1985) denoted to the world a plan of action to ensure their equality in society. The fourth world conference on women held in Beijing in 1995 emphasized the need for **Action for Equality, Development and Peace to ensure** empowerment of women. This conference stressed that "Women need neither crutches nor handouts. They need to be empowered to take their rightful place on an equal footing with men. They need to be liberated from discrimination and exploitation. As if they are not shackled and suppressed in a deliberate manner, women are capable of making greater contribution to the country".

Empowerment through Reservation

The Government of India set up a separate Department of Women and Child Development in 1985 to promote schemes for the development of women and children. The National Perspective Plan on Women (1988) was drawn up for streamlining women issues in policies and programmes and giving them at least one-third share in decision-making bodies from *Panchayats* to the Parliament. The Seventy-Third Amendment Act, 1992 made statutory provisions with regard to the reservation of one-third seats for women in Panchayati Raj institutions. It paved the way for the positive involvement and active participation of women in the development and democratic process of the country. The Panchayati Raj system was evolved primarily to ensure people's participation in the governance of the country and it emphasized the need of women involvement in political process. The participation of women in Panchayati Raj is essential as it helps to empower them to develop their competence so as to enable them to influence and affect the development and decision-making processes at the grassroots level.

The Seventy-Third Amendment Act, 1992 was a significant attempt to revamp Panchayati Raj for decentralization and rural development with a view to grant power to the people at the grassroots level. It has brought a political revolution in India by inserting the provision of reservation for one-third seats for women in the *Panchayats* at three levels for the members as well as chairpersons. It leads to empower the women and enhance their status in society in terms of social, political and economic conditions which facilitate and encourage their participation in the community activities. Certain specific provisions have been incorporated in the Constitution through the Seventy-third Amendment Act to provide representation and to enhance participation of the rural woman in Panchayati Raj institutions. The provisions in the Constitutional Amendment Act "243D (3 and 4) specified that not less than one third (including the number of seats reserved for women belonging to the Scheduled Castes and the Scheduled Tribes) of the total number of seats to be filled by direct election in every *Panchayat*, shall be reserved for women and such seats may be allotted by rotation to different constituencies in a *Panchayat*. The offices of the chairpersons in the *Panchayats* at the village or any other level shall be reserved for the Scheduled Castes, the Scheduled Tribes and women in such a manner, as the legislature of a state may by law provide; provided further that not less than one-third of the total number of offices of chairpersons in the *Panchayats* at each level shall be reserved for women, provided also that the number of offices reserved under this clause shall be allotted by rotation to different *Panchayats* at each levels." All the States in India which fall within the purview of 73rd Amendment have made statutory provisions with regards to the reservation of women in their Panchayati Raj institutions and conducted the elections on the basis of this Act. As a result, there are about one million women elected representatives in rural local bodies. It has opened a new vista for political participation of women folk in rural India.

The reservation system at the grassroots level has opened new horizons for women participation in political activities and is a step forward towards the empowerment of women in Indian society. It is necessary to create social, economic and political conditions for better and effective participation of the women in the local government institutions. However studies conducted in some of the states have, revealed that this empowerment has, by and large, remained formal, as they have not been able to get a share in the decision making process owing to the patriarchal character of India's rural society. These studies have also found that the position of the elected women representatives in the institutions of decentralized rural governance varies from state to state. The prevailing male dominated power structure in villages is generally not ready to accept women as the chairperson of the *Panchayats*. Moreover, women hailing from SC and ST categories find it more difficult to mix with general category representatives in *Panchayats*. Lack of education, political awareness and knowledge of public affairs among women folk of rural areas also discourages the women to attend the meetings and to express their views in panchayats. The social taboos and traditions also create problems in women about induction in these institutions. Therefore there is a need to generate awareness among the women about their rights, capabilities and leadership qualities as well as to sensitize men towards the necessity of women's participation in the local self government institutions so that reservation for women in PR institutions leads to women's political empowerment in real sense. This is the need of the day as women's entry in the rural political system would certainly ensure a change in the political environment of the villages. With the encouragement from the provisions of 73 rd and 74 th Amendments act the non-governmental organisations, political parties and women organisations have been demanding one-third reservation in the parliament and state assemblies which has generated heat in the entire political arenas of the country, and the Central Government was compelled to place the bill in the parliament which could not get through due to the differences and opposition from various political parties. Actually the women reservation bill is a classic case of doublespeak: politicians were endorsing women's reservation in public, but in the back rooms of

Parliament they have been busy sabotaging it. The reasons are clear that the men just do not want to vacate their seats of power. In view of the past experience of placing the bill in the lower house and its opposition the Congress led central government under the pressures has recently placed the bill in the upper house of the parliament.

Recommendations

- Education is an important variable of women empowerment in PR institutions. Therefore, the first and foremost step for empowering women representatives is the removal of illiteracy among them. It should be made obligatory for, both, male as well as female leaders that they must have attained minimum education.

- Comprehensive training programmes can improve the competence and capacities of the women by conducting training camps at local levels. Short duration camps, training work-shops and orientation courses/seminars can be conducted in rural areas to motivate the illiterate women to participate actively in political activities in the rural areas

- There is a need for attitudinal changes among the male members in the families because they can provide women the chance to take part in political activities. The positive and healthy atmosphere must be created in the society by removing social evils like purdah system, dowry, caste-system and other feudal and orthodox traditions in the male dominated rural society.

- It has been observed that male family members of women representatives do not allow them to attend meetings. Therefore, provisions to control the proxy representation by the male family members in the meetings of *Panchayats* need to be made. Women members can be motivated to attend the meetings regularly by giving them honorarium and TA/DA.

- Stern action should be taken against such persons who create caste and communal feelings. The upper castes' representatives can be educated to bring attitudinal changes. Legal provisions can also be made to bring them at par with the general categories representatives effectively.

- The voluntary agencies, social and women organizations can play a significant role in generating political awakening among women folk, in general, and women leaders, in particular.

- The governmental agencies should make wide publicity to motivate the rural women to participate in *Panchayat* activities by means of public meetings, pamphlets, booklets, audio-visual aids and advertisements through print and electronic media.

- It has been found that the course syllabi at primary and high levels do not give any stress on the role of women in society and the equality of sexes. It is, therefore, suggested that the courses should be designed to inculcate the feelings of equality and responsibility among girls even from the tender age to enable them to participate in public affairs.

- Last but not the least, there is an urgent need of co-operative and positive attitude of bureaucracy towards women empowerment of PR institutions.

References

Biju, M.R., (1997) *Potitics of Democracy and Decentralization in India* (A case study of Kerala), Atlantic Publishers.

Chahar, S.S.(ed), (2005) *Governance at Grassroots Level in India*, Kanishka Publishers New Delhi.

Gupta, U.N., (2006) *Human Rights (Vol.-I)*, Atlantic Publishers, New Delhi.

Jayapalan, N. (2000) *Women Studies*, Atlantic Publishers, New Delhi.

__________(2000) *Human Rights*, Atlantic Publishers, New Delhi.

__________(2001) *Women and Human Right*, Atlantic Publishers, New Delhi.

Mohanty Bedabati; (2005) *Violence against Women: An Analysis of Contemporary Realities*; Kanshik Publishers, New Delhi.

Narula, Uma, (2005) *Indian Women Across Generations*: Atlantic Publishers, New Delhi.

Palai, Arun Kumar, (1999) National Human Rights Commission of India: *Formation, Functioning and Future Prospects*, Atlantic Publishers, New Delhi.

Singh, Baldev, (1996) *Decentralization Panchayati Raj and District Planning*, Atlantic Publishers, New Delhi.

Srinivas, M.N. (1966) *Social Change in Modern India*, Allied Publishers, Bombay.

2

Social and Economic Empowerment of Women in India

Jyoti Tiwari

Social status of women

In most of the traditional societies generally women had always been at a disadvantage. Their education was limited to learning domestic skills and they had no access to positions of power. Marriage was almost the necessity as a means of support or protection and pressure was usually to produce children especially male heirs. The age of enlightenment with its egalitarian political emphasis and industrial revolution brought about enormous economic and social changes. During the industrial revolution, the transformation of handicrafts in to machine powered mass production, meant that women could become wage earners in the new factories. This was the beginning of their independence. This helped to expand the role of women out of the home to factories and offices. In the late 18th century women's rights movement also known as feminism started in Europe. After which the status of women began to change and by late 19th century the women throughout the world had gained many rights. However the complete political, economical and social equality with men still remains to be achieved. The feminist movement in India may find its genesis in the report on status of women, which was published in the year 1975. The report on the status of women was prepared on the request of United Nations, by the member nations for the Mexico conference on the status of women, held in 1975. The Mexico conference and the publication of the report on the status of women in India led to a number of conferences and seminars to discuss the issues related to the women and also the women's movement in India.

The principle of gender equality is enshrined in Indian constitution in its preamble, fundamental duties and rights and directive principles. The constitution not only grants equality to women but also empowers the states to adopt measures of positive discrimination in women's favour. From the fifth five-year plan (1974-78) onwards there has been a marked shift in the approach to women's issues from welfare to development. The National women's Commission was set up by an act of parliament in 1990 to safeguard the rights and legal entitlements of women. However, there still exists a wide gap between the goals enunciated in the constitution, policies, plans and programs on the one hand and the situational reality of the status of women in India, on the other. On the basis of the situation of women's participation in economic agenda in India, the world economic forum's report has put the country among the bottom 10. The forum's latest gender gap index report puts India among the world's 20 worst countries for gender bias. In view of this the women in India have a long way to go as far as women empowerment is concerned. Actually India's paradox is that prosperity and progress have done nothing to change the view that a girl child is a burden, as well as an investment without return. The all India sex ratio is 927 girls for 1000 boys which is worse than the country like Nigeria (965) and Pakistan (958). The pressure on women to bear sons coupled with the easy availability of the techniques of sex determination is actually responsible for growing number of missing girl children. For those girls who some how stay alive and do make it out of the womb, survival isn't a guarantee as many die in their infancy because they are given less nutrition and medical care. They get less education both in quality and quantity as compared to their male counterparts. Actually India being a patriarchal society glorifies virtues of patience, morality and sacrifice in women and keeps them over occupied in child rearing practices and domestic chores.

Though there are many laws to protect women and also for empowering them but real empowerment of women is possible only if they are given proper access to health care, quality education at all levels, safety at work place as well as at home, social security and an environment free from any kind of discrimination. Though women constitute more than one third of the world's labour force, but generally they remain concentrated in a limited number of traditional occupations, many of which are usually low paid. The latest ILO report says that "more women are working than ever before but they are more likely than men to get low productivity, low paid and vulnerable jobs." (ILO, 2008) It is a well-known fact that women are the main contributors in agriculture sector especially in hill areas but despite toiling from dawn to dusk their economic contribution generally remains unrecognized and unpaid. As the men migrate to cities in search of jobs, many rural women are left behind to support their families and agriculture alone. In the absence of the male members women could generally be found engaged in farming operations, raising livestock, cutting fodder and bringing fuel and water from distant places which keeps them so busy that they do not find time to indulge in other activities of their choice. In such situation the empowerment of women also seems to be a distant dream and their status in the society still low.

Health and nutritional status of the women

India has made a considerable progress in social and economic development in recent decades, as the improvement in life expectancy, infant mortality and literacy demonstrates it. However, improvement in women's health, particularly in hills have lagged behind gains in other areas. Health status of Indian women especially in rural areas is very poor. Females experience more episodes of illness than males and are less likely to receive medical treatment before the illness is well advanced. In India it is widely prevalent custom that men folk eat first, children next and women last. (Devadas, 1974) Thus, women's health and nutritional status is bound by social and cultural factors also. Numerous studies point towards the fact that malnutrition is serious health concern for the Indian women (Chatterjee, 1990; Desai, 1994). Studies have also indicated that women do not get adequate nutrition during pregnancy and lactation. Due to which India accounts for nearly 25 percent of world's maternal deaths. Every year about 1,25,000 Indian women die from pregnancy related causes and malnutrition. To eliminate malnutrition over long term, there is a need to consider the important underlying gender issues, which constrain women's capabilities and capacities. Even in this age of progress and growth many poor women still lack the authority to make decisions regarding household resources and affairs and depend on the male members for any decisions. Girls are forced to marry during adolescent years, leading to early pregnancies, poorer birth outcomes and poor nutritional status. Women also lack control over the decisions related to reproduction. Actually women are the one who need health and nutrition education more as well as control over their body and related rights. Being homemakers and nurtures their knowledge, awareness and efforts would have a marked impact on health and nutritional status of other family members also.

Violence against women

Despite the legal safeguards provided for the physical and mental security of the women, violence against women is increasing day by day in our country. Women are neither safe inside their homes nor out side the home. Violence against women manifests itself as rape, molestation, eve teasing, kidnapping, domestic violence such as wife battering, dowry harassment, dowry death, cruelty to women driving them to commit suicide or other forms of violence like female feticide, female infanticide, child marriages and child abuse. Social stereotyping and violence at the domestic and social levels are very common in the society. Actually the lower status accorded to women in family and society results in gender based violence and due to these laws can also do little unless there is a change in cultural and social values and mind set of the society towards the women.

In India female sex ratio is continuously declining. Despite laws banning tests to determine the sex of the unborn child, the killing of female fetus is common in India. According to United Nations report nearly 2000 unborn girls are illegally aborted every day in India. In a recent study conducted by a team of pediatricians from Delhi's St. Stephens Hospital it was found that there has been sharp decline in the sex ratio after 1980 i.e. after the arrival of ultra-sonography technique. The study also shows that a girl child is welcome in the family only if the family already has son to carry on the family name and then her presence is regarded as maintaining balance in the family. In the absence of a son parents often have no qualms about doing away with the unborn daughter. In a recent development the Supreme Court of India on 25th October 2007 has directed all the states and union territories to bring in suitable laws to make registration of all marriages compulsory to safeguard the women from any kind of cheating and misbehaviour by the husbands. This is a praiseworthy step for the protection of women's rights. This will surely reduce the exploitation of women, incidence of child marriages, polygamy and desertion of wife after marriage.

Strategies for social and economic empowerment of women

Women constitute nearly half the population and the social justice also demands equal participation in all the socio-economic processes. Development of the nation is hampered if half of its population lags behind whether in political participation or in socio-economic processes. Though the upper class and middle class educated women particularly in cities who are working and getting good salary packages generate an impression that the status of Indian women has changed. But majority of lower class women and women of rural areas still suffer social and economic oppression in silence. There is a need to plan strategies for such women and their real empowerment. Social and economic empowerment of women can be achieved through the following ways:

- Eradication of Social evils like child marriages, child labour, purdah system; dowry system, which stands in the way of women's development and empowerment.

- Providing access to following
  - (a) Access to education
  - (b) Access to health and nutrition
  - (c) Access to water and sanitation

- Since education is the most important agent in improving status of women and generating awareness about their rights, family planning, and developing courage to fight against inequality therefore greater emphasis should be on female literacy, economic independence of women, health and nutritional education, access to the girl child to primary and secondary education, to reduce the drop out rate of girls and provision of guidance and counseling services for the girls.

- Shortage of female teachers poses a major barrier for girls' schooling in rural areas hence more female teachers must be appointed in rural areas.

- Making self-help groups for sharing and discussing the broad social, legal, political and economic issues, which affect their lives, like family planning, the number of children they should have and spacing between births, domestic violence and child marriages etc.

- Participation of girls in non-traditional courses and their involvement in science and technology must be encouraged. Promoting and ensuring vocational training for girls to enhance immediate utility of educating them.

- Creating new avenues for employment of women and upgrading their existing employment conditions.

- Expansion of small-scale industries to create potential for employment. Development of skills and income generating activities like pickle making, fish processing, embroidery, garment making and other skills. The earnings through such income generating schemes would definitely improve the self-confidence and self esteem of the women.

- Laws related to the protection of women's rights must be strictly enforced and laws must be made against any form of violence against women like female feticide, female infanticide, child marriages and child abuse.

- It is essential to sensitize the entire law enforcement machinery to gender issues particularly violence against women.

- Elimination of all forms of discrimination against women and considering men and women as equally worthy human beings with dignity.

- Promoting positive role of mass media to portray balanced picture of women and to communicate social messages and creating national debate on issues like women's equality and empowerment.

- Improving farming practices and diversification of agriculture. Programs of non-conventional sources of energy like solar energy, biogas, and use of smokeless chulhas must be encouraged to improve and change the life style of rural women.

- Promoting social awareness and discussions on gender issues and women's rights. Changing the mindsets of people and acceptance of women in work roles is much more important because over hundreds of years men have dominated the social structure, therefore they would not readily accept the success of women.

- Attitude of women themselves also needs to be shaped to creative and positive thinking.

- Increased participation of women in political structure

- Reviewing of curriculum and educational materials to include gender education and human rights issues.

- For social empowerment, working women must have an environment, which frees them from the tensions of childcare and permits them to give their best to their profession. For this woman needs support services to enable them to balance their household and professional duties. Facility of crèches or childcare centers can be very helpful in this regard.

- Safe housing facilities must be provided for working women, female students and trainees. There is a need to give special assistance to women who are living in extreme poverty, destitute women, affected by natural calamities, disabled women and those who are the victim of marital violence. Efforts need to be made for their rehabilitation.

References

Bagchi, Jashodhara (Ed) 2003: Indian Women Myth and Reality. Orient and Longman.

Begum,S.M.(2000). Human Rights in India: Issues and perspectives, New Delhi. A.P.H. Publishing Corporation.

Chatterjee, Meera, (1990) Indian Women: Their Health and Economic Productivity, World Bank Discussion Papers 109, Washington, DC.

Desai, Sonalde (1994) Gender Inequalities and Demographic Behaviour, India.

Devadas, R.P. (1974) Social and Economic Dimensions of Nutrition. Proceedings of the Nutrition Society of India. 17: 66-72.

Dwaipayan Ghosh: All Skewed up for Second Girl Child. Times of India. New Delhi. September 25, 2007.

http:// nutritionfoundationofindia.

http://wcd.nic.in/empwomen.htm

ILO 2008. Global employment trends for women, Times of India, New Delhi. March 9,2008.

Kumar, A (1991). Human Resource Development: An Interdisciplinary Approach, New Delhi. Anmol Publications.

Madan, G.K.(2002) Indian Rural Women's Problems. New Delhi. Radha Publications.

Microsoft Encarta Encyclopedia

Neelam Raaj: Son-rise but deficit of Girls. The Times of India. New Delhi. March 8, 2008.

Pachauri, S.K.(1999)Women and Human Rights. New Delhi. A.P.H. Publishing Corporation.

The Times of India. New Delhi. November 12, 2007.

3

Women Empowerment in Uttarakhand: Prospects and Challenges

Annpurna Nautiyal

Uttarakhand is one of the new states of Indian Union which came into existence in November 2000 on account of the pressures generated by a long mass movement by its people. This was the movement in which people of all walks of life participated spontaneously because they believed that their concerns for development, employment generation, resource availability, equitable distribution of services and facilities etc would be resolved in an efficient manner by their own state. Women from the remotest corner of Uttarakhand, though not knowing the actual benefits; became active partners in this movement as they believed that the movement for the creation of a separate Uttarakhand state under the Indian Union was necessary for the welfare of their children, community and society as well as to provide relief from continued underdevelopment, neglect and apathy. They were optimistic that their own state would not only reduce some of their miseries but also have solutions for their problems related to their sustenance. However, women who played an active role in this movement and made all kinds of sacrifices were not given their due after the creation of this state; rather they were pushed to the side lanes. It is ironical that in a state which was created to satisfy the demands of the holistic development of the area and also to bring the people in to the national main stream, the condition and the quality of life of the woman of the remote hill areas has not improved at all. Although the women of this hill state do share more or less the same plight being shared by their counterparts in other rural areas of India but the magnitude of their drudgery is very high due to the geographical and ecological conditions of this area. The tough and some times hostile terrain, adverse weather conditions, rugged mountains, scarcity of cultivable land, paucity of basic facilities like water, electricity, medical, non availability of fuel, fodder and water near their homes snatches peace, comfort and ease from their life. The lack of proper knowledge and general awareness do not allow the women to even take benefit of the rights given to all the women of India by its constitution and make use of their potential and tremendous talent. An attempt has been made in this paper to analyze the problems being faced by the hill women and their prospects of becoming the active and empowered partners in the developmental process and the political institutions. The analysis is mainly based on the findings of the field survey conducted in the three blocks of Disrtict Chamoli Garhwal in Uttarakhand.

Administrative and Demographical Profile of Uttarakhand

With a population of 84,79,562 and an area of 53,483 sq. km Uttarakhand is located in the North- West part of India between 28 ⁰ 44'-31 ⁰ 25 N' and 77⁰ 35'-81⁰ '2' E. The following table provides the district wise details of the Tahseal and Vikaskhand (Blocks) and population of Uttarakhand.

Table I - Uttarakhand District wise area Tahseal and Vikashkand (Blocks)

S.N.	*State / District*	*Area(Sq. Km.)*	*Tahseal*	*Vikashkhand (Block)*	*Population*
1	Almora	3074	3	11	630446
2	Nainital	4767	5	8	7629 12
3	Pithoragad	7218	5	8	462149
4	Bageshwar	2311	2	3	249453
5	Champawat	1638	1	4	224461
6	Udham Singh Nagar	2027	4	7	1234548
7	Chamoli	7626	6	9	369198
8	Uttarkashi	8016	4	6	294179
9	Pauri	5397	5	15	696851
10	Tehri	3796	5	9	604608
11	Dehradun	3088	4	6	1279083
12	Rudraprayag	2252	2	3	227461
13	Haridwar	1994	3	6	1444213
	Total	**53,483**	**49**	**95**	**8479562**

Source: Census 2001: India 2003. Ministry of Information and Broadcasting, Government of India and Sankhiyki Patrika, Arth and Sankhya Nidashyala, Uttarakhand, 2004.

As the above table shows that there are 49 Tahseals and 95 blocks in Uttarakhand. Some of the districts like Dehradun (which is also the capital of Uttarakhand) and Nainital are famous for their renowned public schools as well as infrastructural facilities. Nainital is also a well-known hill station and visited by the tourists frequently. Other districts are still struggling for development, infrastructural facilities and most of the hill districts are even not connected by rail services. Due to the poor condition of roads and communication net work some of the areas are still very backward in terms of

Table II - District wise population, sex ratio and population density in Uttarakhand

S.N.	*District*	*Population*			*Sex ratio (per 1000 male)*	*Density (2001)*
		Total People	*Male*	*Female*		
1	Almora	630446	293576	336870	1147	205
2	Nainital	7629 12	400336	362576	906	198
3	Pithoragarh	462149	227592	234557	1031	65
4	Bageshwar	249453	118202	131251	1110	108
5	Champawat	224461	110916	113545	1024	126
6	Udham Singh Nagar	1234548	649020	585528	902	424
7	Chamoli	369198	183033	186165	1017	48
8	Uttarkashi	294179	151599	142580	941	37
9	Pauri	696851	331138	365713	1104	129
10	Tehri	604608	294842	309766	1051	148
11	Dehradun	1279083	675549	603534	893	414
12	Rudraprayag	227461	107425	120036	11 17	120
13	Haridwar	1444213	773173	671040	868	612
	Total	**8479562**	**4316401**	**4163161**	**964**	**159**

Source: Census 2001: India 2003. *Ministry of Information and Broadcasting, Government of India*, P. 816-817 and Madhumod K. Raijada: *Uttaranchal Eak Adhyan*, Sahtiya Bhawan Publications, Agra, 2002, p. 15.

facilities like schools, medical facilities, water, electricity etc. There are schools but no proper buildings, facilities and teachers, there are hospitals but without doctors, medicines and equipments. In view of this the main agenda of the government is how to provide basic facilities to all and to fulfill the aspirations of its people.

The district wise population, sex ratio and population density has been given in the Table II. Udham Singh Nagar in Kumaun Mandal and Hardwar and some areas of Dehradun of Garhwal Mandal fall in the plain areas of Uttarakhand and rest of the districts in hill areas. Udham Singh Nagar, Haridwar and Dehradun are the most populous areas with high density of population. The density of population in Uttarkashi and Chamoli in Garhwal Mandal and Pithoragarh in Kumaun Mandal is the lowest.

Empowerment and Women's life in the Hill Areas of Garhwal Himalayas: Issues of Concerns

In the rural and remote hill areas of Garhwal Himalayas women are still leading a very tough life not only due to the tough geographical conditions but due to the host of other various problems. For example, agriculture, which is the mainstay of the 80 percent people of Garhwal Himalayas is highly unproductive because of the small agricultural fields, fragmented and scattered land holdings, lack of irrigation facilities and prevalence of traditional methods and practices of crop. In the absence of other means of suitable employment in the remote areas, the out-migration of the male population for the search of employment becomes a necessary survival strategy. The migration of the male population to the cities has converted the hill economy into a money order economy as the families sustain themselves on the basis of the remittance sent by them. Male migration besides increasing women's responsibilities has also produced imbalance in the male- female population because as a result of the migration of the young and able bodied males only the aged, the women and children are left behind to look after the agriculture, animals and other activities. The migration of the young male population on the one hand increases the miseries, socio, economic and physical burden of the women of the Garhwal Himalayas on the other; it also enhances their work load drastically. Because whenever a male member of a household migrates his responsibilities and tasks are automatically transferred to his wife or the other female members of the family. The women in hills are estimated to contribute between 55 to 60 percent of the total labour and perform almost all the agricultural activities. Their work load generally comes around 16-17 hours. According to the leading development economist and former director of the United Nations Development Programmes (UNDP) the late Mahbub ul Haq "The real wealth of a nation is its people. And the purpose of development is to create an enabling environment for people to enjoy long, healthy, and creative lives, however, this simple but powerful truth is too often forgotten in the pursuit of material and financial wealth by all". In view of this definition of development if we look at the situation of the women of Garhwal Himalayas we find that even after the creation of the Uttarakhand the women are still deprived of the basic needs . What could be more ironical than the fact the women of the hill areas have to still cover a distance of 2-3 kilometers on foot every day to obtain water, fodder and fuel and carry load on their back. Nothing concrete has been done by the governments to save the women from this daily drudgery and bring significant change in the daily life style of the women. As a result of this the women have little time to engage in socio-political activities or to be trained in skill improving activities which could be helpful in their empowerment.

Political Empowerment, Representation and Participation of Women

Women have been given equal rights for their empowerment by the Indian constitution; articles 14 to 16 provide for equal rights to men and women and prohibit any kind of discrimination. Articles 39 and 42 provide for equal means of livelihood, equal pay for equal work, just and humane conditions of work and maternity relief to the women. For encouraging women's participation and empowerment at the grass root level 1/3 seats have also been reserved for them in Panchayats and local bodies. Domestic violence has been made a punishable offence under protection of women from domestic violence law (2005). In 2004-2005 the Ministry of Women and Child Development also adopted 'Budgeting for Gender Equity' as its mission statement and 2005-06 was devoted as a year to carry forward this aim.(Yojana, October, 2006) The Eighth five year plan (1992-97) accepted the need to ensure a definite flow of funds from the general development sectors to women. The Ninth Plan (1997-2002) adopted the Women's Component Plan as one of the major strategies and directed both the central and the state governments to ensure 30 percent funds for women related sectors. Tenth plan reinforced the gender budgeting to establish its gender differential impact and to translate gender commitments into budgetary commitments. (Nagaraj, 2006) These measures and timely initiatives taken by the government sound very progressive and reflect the movement of women from being an oppressed category to the empowered category as these provisions have allowed women to become part of the developmental process and be empowered. However, the educated and resource rich women of the urban areas are generally taking advantage of these measures because in the rural areas particularly in the hill areas, the heavy work load, lack of quality education, resources, awareness, gender disparity and discrimination is still prohibiting the women to take advantage of these. Their ignorance about the clauses of equality and empowerment impinges on their productivity in social and political arena. With the result only a handful of women with links with the important people or top political families could so far made their mark in Indian politics. Women who come from a different background always find it very difficult to rise to the top without the support of a god father or mentor. It is rather paradoxical that the political parties who claim to be a supporter of gender equality generally refrain from fielding women candidates in a large number in assembly or Lok Sabha elections because of the fear of loosing the seats. Even in a new state like Uttarakhand for which the women along with the youth and others fought a long battle during the Uttarakhand movement as Matra Shakti, no preferential treatment has been given to them in politics. In the second assembly elections of Uttarakhand state held in February 2007 only a few women were given tickets to contest the election by the main political parties. Thus the Congress party gave tickets to only six women candidates, Bhartiya Janta Party (BJP) fielded seven women candidates, Uttarakhand Kranti Dal (UKD) gave tickets to four women, Samajwadi Party (SP) and Bahujan Samaj Wadi Party (BSP) fielded two candidates each and the National Congress Party and Bhartiya Janshakti Party also gave only one ticket each to the women candidates. Despite the increased number of the female voters and vote share only 03 women from the BJP and 01 from congress party out of the 52 women contestants could make it to the state legislature. However, the scenario of women's political participation and activism at the grass root level has changed slightly with the implementation of the 33 percent reservation for the women in the local bodies and Panchayati Raj Institutions.

Impact of Reservation on Women in Local Bodies

The reservation of 1/3 seats at the grass root level in the Panchayati Raj institutions for the women by provisions of the 73 rd and 74 th amendment can be assumed as the real effort for increasing women's participation in the political process. With such provisions women have now started to take interest in the political process and their level of awareness is also increasing. There are women who have taken advantage of this reservation and by their dedication and sincerity for implementing the various schemes have registered their presence and also made a difference in delivering the results. Their work in improvising the facilities in schools, water tanks, roads, distribution of funds to the right people and working for the cause of the women has been commendable. It has also been reported that in the villages where educated and literate women had been acting as the Village Pradhan (Head of the village political body) the level of corruption and delay in implementing the schemes had been reducing as they had clear ideas about the problems and their resolution. Due to their inherent qualities the women generally think about the welfare of the people therefore, the meetings of the Gram Panchayats and women's participation in them was also found to be increasing as the women find it easier to discuss their problems with the women head of the Panchayat. (Dogra 2001) As women have an inclination to focus on fundamental developmental issues like roads, drinking water and schools than on high-flying projects therefore it is being felt in a large section that bringing women in larger numbers into the legislative bodies both in the states and at the Centre would certainly improve the working of these bodies.

However, the coin has other side also because the women who participate in the election have to face a tough ordeal. The foremost problem which they face comes from their homes, from their husbands, father in laws or other senior members because the senior members of the family consider politics a dirty world which is not at all suitable for the women. Even the women who are able to get the permission from their family face the opposition from other men of the society. The disagreeing powerful men of the villages not only keep a sharp eye on their work, but also always try to humiliate or let down them. Sometimes women are also found to be suffering from the conservativeness and complexes of considering themselves inferior to men. In the studies of the panchayat system in India especially by Niraja Jayal and Nirmala Buch, (Jayal 2000 and Buch 2000) it has been reported that women are persistently mocked, humiliated and devalued in the panchayats if they are illiterate while the illiterate men do not face such humiliation. Such disparity and attitude towards women also demoralizes the women and despite potential they remain unable to deliver the results. Women often act as stand-ins for their husbands who are unable to hold their seats due to some political or other reasons, in such cases also if the women are illiterate they generally work as a proxy to their husbands but if they are literate they can easily become capable of doing their work independently. If a woman seeks to contest a non-reserved seat her chances of winning and working independently tend to increase if she has a potential to move as a self-sufficient actor in society, with access to communications and information. (Nussbaum, 2002) Literacy and education are therefore considered crucial in such transition of woman from a house wife to a political leader or empowered woman. Due to the provisions of the empowerment and women's growing role in local bodies it has been found that now the women are getting more inclined to provide education to their daughters so that they can take their place as equals in the new system. Besides political empowerment women's literacy is also crucial, for their access to the legal system, population control as well as improving their bargaining position in the family. In view of it can be said that the literate and educated women can make a difference in the socio-political arena, improve their position in the society. It is therefore, necessary to provide more facilities to the women for education, training and improving their skills and they also need to be motivated to participate in the political process in a large number.

To assess the situation of the women and to relate her problems with the above picture a field survey was conducted and the findings of the survey has been explained in the following text.

Study area and profile of the sample

For assessing the ground reality and the position of the women three blocks and twelve villages falling under these blocks in the district Chamoli Garhwal were selected for a field survey. In Tharali block of Chamoli Garhwal Chaproan, Keera, Bajwar and Devrada, in Deval block Icholi, Jhalia, Lawandi and Torti and in Gairsain block Kheti, Randoli, Sarkot and Chimta villages were taken and a total number of 330 women respondents (consisting of all caste segments) in these villages were selected randomly to get a first hand idea of the condition, quality of life, facilities, level of awareness, activism, empowerment and participation on the basis of their professional status, family structure, martial status, age, monthly income, facilities at home, distance from road head, caste, educational status, participation in political and social issues etc.

Respondents were classified into two age groups from 18 to 40 years and 40 years and above. 187 respondents belonged to 18-40 age group and 143 belonged to 40 and above age group. Out of 330 respondents 287 women were house wives and 43 were involved in other activities (like students, employed, private business, etc). 290 women were married and rest was single. 187 women lived in nuclear families whereas 143 lived in joint families. 117 women were found to be illiterate, 160 were literate, 33 respondents had education up to intermediate level and 20 had education up to bachelor and above. 33 percent respondents had a monthly family income of Rs. 2000, the monthly family income of 46.5 per cent respondents was around Rs. 4000 and 20.5 per cent earned a monthly income of Rs. 4000. 60 per cent respondents were located at a distance of 3 kilometers from the road head, 18 per cent lived at a distance of 4 to 6 kilometers from the road head and 22 per cent were located at a distance of 6 kilometers from the road head. 6 per cent respondents belonged to the Brahmin caste, 83 per cent Rajput caste, 6 percent scheduled caste and 3 per cent scheduled tribes (23, 277, 20 and 10 respectively).

Methodology

To be acquainted with the level of socio-political awareness and knowledge of the women of these remotely situated villages questions related to social problems, voting preferences and participation in elections, name of the political leaders of the state, national leaders, Prime minister, local Member of Legislative Assembly, Parliament, information about the various governmental schemes for rural areas, national and international events, participation in the solution of local problems, meaning of empowerment, involvement in the NGO or any other village based group, participation in different movements, political activism, position and say in family decision making, role in society, level of education etc. were asked through the structured questionnaires. The data was also collected through interviews as well as personal observations during the course of the field survey.

Observations and Analysis

The survey revealed that the level of awareness of the house wives' about the social and political issues was 33.06 percent whereas the level of awareness about these issues among the unmarried, employed and students was 66.94 percent. The house wives were found to be less aware about the political issues and the names of the MP, MLA etc. than the employed, students and unmarried women as the later segment had more chances of meeting and interacting with other people, groups, accessing news through a variety of sources like newspapers, electronic media and also participating in the meetings organised by the various societies, institutions etc. The house wives also exhibited a kind of dependence on their husbands or other male members for replying to the questions related to their rights, names of the MLA or MP, meaning of reservation etc. as they were not certain about the answers. They were also found to be suffering from a kind of inferiority complex and some what reluctant to share their views about the contemporary social and political issues but some of the women of older generation were found to be more vocal on the declining values among the young generation. Young people in the 18-40 age groups were found to be more aware about the burning socio and political issues. Their level of awareness about the social and political issues was found to be 70.49 per cent but in the 40 and above age group the level of social awareness among the respondents was found to be 29.51 per cent. The level of awareness about social and political issues like participation in the Uttarakhand movement or the present situation or the issue of shifting of the capital in 18-40 groups was 49 per cent and 14.05 per cent, and awareness about economic and environmental issues like knowledge about the Chipko Movement for environmental protection, environmental degradation, biosphere reserves etc. was 20.67 per cent and 16.28 per cent.

It was also found that most of the educated and employed women belonged to the young age group (18-40) as stated above that awareness is also linked to education which is a mechanism for changing the mind set consequently, as the level of education grows the graph of awareness also raises. It was found that most of the unmarried women were engaged either in the higher or intermediate education therefore, their level of awareness was higher than the married women. Although there is no denying the fact that the attitude of differentiating between boy and girl is present in the urban educated families also but they take interest in their education also. But in the remote hill areas as the onus of all the activities lies on the women therefore, if any assistance or helping hand is required the daughters are asked to look after the younger siblings and household chores even at the cost of their schooling. The traditional mind set of differentiating between a boy and a girl can be said to be responsible for the deprivation and exploitation of the women and girls and their low and poor quality of education and literacy. During our survey it was also found that a large number of girls and boys were only educated up to class ninth because they could not pass their high school examinations even after many attempts. On being asked its reason it was told that the syllabus of high school was not only difficult but in the absence of good and competent teachers in the schools the students find it difficult to comprehend the science subjects. In place of attempting again to clear the exam they usually prefer to run away from their homes to the cities and find small jobs like cleaning or cooking in some small hotel etc. and the failure on the part of girls means early marriage for them.

However, this does not suggest that the parents particularly the mothers are not in favour of educating their daughters, they are aware of the advantages and also wish that their daughters should not face the hardship like them but it was accepted by the women that the lack of helping hand and enormity of work forces them to take the unpleasant decision of asking their daughters to baby sit or drop from the school.

Awareness about issues is also related to the economic condition of the family therefore, the women from a good income family also showed a higher level of awareness than the women of less income group family as the higher income group had resources to own and get information from the facilities like TV, news papers etc. On the other hand the women from low income families were found to be busy or more worried about the mundane affairs or sustaining the day today needs of the family and due to which they did not exhibit any interest towards acquiring the information about the social, political or other issues. The distance of the residence from the road head has also produced difference in the level of awareness of the women because the more the distance from the road head the availability of the means of accessing information and increasing knowledge was found to be decreasing. The habitants of such areas were found to not only having less regular contact with the people of other areas but also fewer means of knowledge and information as well as social and political meetings due to the remoteness and inaccessibility of their area. Such situation was mostly prevailing in the areas which were located at a distance of 6 or more kilometers from the road head. These areas were also found to be lagging behind in terms of basic facilities like water, electricity, cooking gas, schools, education facilities, health facilities and other means of modern living.

In India since the beginning generally the awareness, information and knowledge has always been associated to the caste composition in the society due to which among the people of higher caste (Brahmin and Rajput) of the society the level of education, awareness has always been high in comparison to the people belonging to the lower caste segments. Although in the survey area the general level of awareness about all the issues among the women of all caste was found to be low however, the level of awareness among Brahmins and Rajputs (high caste section of the society) was 40 per cent and 33.38 per cent, and among the lower caste segments, i.e., S.C. (Scheduled Caste) and S.T. (Scheduled Tribes) it was only 24.62 per cent. These sections were found to be lagging behind because of their poverty, lack of education, and resources. It was also found that as majority of these sections did not own the agricultural land and other resources, they had been mostly working as agricultural labour therefore as soon as they get some employment they tend to migrate from the village and thus only the very poor families with women members are left behind to cope with the domestic as well as agriculture work. The women of these sections were mostly found ignorant and deprived of their rights because of the low level of awareness, interest, literacy, and lack of self -esteem, self-confidence, time and poor economic conditions.

Empowerment: Reality and Constraints in the Hill Areas

In the rural and remote hill areas of Uttarakhand on the one hand it was found that the women have neither time nor are they provided support by the men to be part of the political process therefore most of the women did not show any interest towards politics, political parties or political participation. But on the other hand, it was also found that although the women are not fully aware of the provisions of 73rd and 74th amendments but they are entering into the Panchayats by taking the benefit of the 33 percent reservation given to them in these institutions. However in the absence of the knowledge about their rights and duties in these institutions, it has also been found that in some of the cases the husbands had been playing important role in the Panchayats. It was reported in the local media that in the general body meeting (Dainik Jagaran 2004, August 3) of the Chamoli District Panchayat in place of the woman member her husband came to attend the meeting. It reflects that women are still giving their right to their husbands or the other men or they prefer to be guided or dictated by their husbands or the male members. This condition appears only when the women are illiterate, unable to fulfill their rights and sufferings from some complex or the men are against their participation in such bodies and want to confine her in the home affairs only. Such women actually are the ones for whom the word empowerment has no meaning as they remain unable to reap its benefits because of their ignorance and complexes and act as a rubber stamp for their husbands. Such women had no knowledge about the rights and duties given to them by the provisions of the 73 and 74 amendment acts and their understanding about reservation and these provisions was limited to contesting election for these therefore, most of the answers related to their role and functions in the Panchyats were given by their husbands. Though these cases are rare and there is a change in the situation with the reservation of the 1/3 seats in the local bodies but still much needs to be done to improve the ground reality as it was also found during the survey that in some places instead of the women head of the village Panchyat her husband was being addressed as Pradhan Ji and the works being done in the village from the Panchyat funds

Table III. Details of Male- Female Representation of Village Pradhan Blockwise in District Chamoli (Garhwal)

Name of Block	*Total Pradhan*	*F*	*M*	*General*		*SC*		*OBC*		*ST*	
				F	*M*	*F*	*M*	*F*	*M*	*F*	*M*
Karanprayag	86	28	58	18	48	10	10	-	0	0	0
Pokhri	71	23	48	18	40	5	8	-	0	0	0
Narayanbagur	62	23	39	16	33	6	6	1	0	0	0
Tharali	50	17	33	16	24	1	7	-	2	0	0
Dewal	44	15	29	12	23	3	6	0	0	0	0
Gairsain	86	31	55	23	47	7	8	1	0	0	0
Ghat	46	16	30	11	24	4	6	1	0	0	0
Dasoli	58	21	37	13	28	7	8	-	1	1	1
Joshimath	49	18	31	9	19	2	4	-	0	7	7
Total	552	192	360	136	286	45	60	3	2	8	8

(F-Female, M-Male, SC-Scheduled Castes, OBC-Other Backward Castes, ST-Scheduled Tribes. This table is based on the data of 2003 election of panchayats).

Table IV- Details of Village Pradhan's Educational Qualification Block wise in District Chamoli Garhwal

Name of Block	*Female*						*Male*					
	P	*J*	*HS*	*Inter*	*UG*	*PG*	*P*	*J*	*HS*	*Inter*	*UG*	*PG*
Karanprayag	14	3	5	1	4	1	14	14	11	7	6	6
Pokhri	11	6	2	1	1	2	7	11	12	4	7	7
Narayanbagur	13	4	3	-	3	-	9	7	10	6	4	3
Tharali	8	4	1	2	2	-	4	11	6	5	2	5
Dewal	7	6	-	2	-	-	5	9	7	5	1	2
Gairsain	17	3	4	5	1	1	20	12	14	6	2	1
Ghat	11	3	1	1	-	-	6	5	8	4	2	5
Dasoli	9	3	3	2	3	1	3	11	-	7	7	9
Joshimath	10	2	1	2	1	2	4	5	3	9	4	6
Total	100	34	20	16	15	7	72	85	71	53	35	44

(P- Primary, J-Junior, HS-High School, Intermediate, U.G.-Under Graduate, P.G.-Post Graduate)

Source: Both the tables have been compiled on the basis of data collected from the different blocks and the office of the Panchayat Raj Adhikari and based on the data of the 2003 election.

were also being looked after by him. These cases may be said to be exceptional but to overcome such pathetic examples it becomes more than important to conduct training courses and awareness generating programmes regularly so that women could become empowered in the real sense of the term. In Uttarakhand after the formation of the new state elections for the Panchayati Raj institutions were held in 2003. The details of the male-female representation of the village pradhans and their educational qualification in Chamoli district has been presented in the Tables III and IV.

As shown in Table III and IV out of a total number of 552 Village Pradhans 192 females and 360 males had been holding the post of village pradhan. 136 women belonged to general categories, 45 belonged the scheduled caste category and 3 in OBC and 8 in the Scheduled Tribe category. In Karnprayag, Pokhari, Tharali, Ghat and Dasoli block no women belonged to the OBC category. In most of the blocks no Scheduled Tribes women were found to be holding the post of the village pradhan. The detail of the educational status of the village pradhans have been presented in Table IV.

As the Table IV shows that in some blocks like Tharali, Dewal and Dasoli the number of primary educated women even could not cross the double digit mark however it is a also a sign of relief that no female Pradhan was found to be illiterate. Most of them had education up to primary level (up to class 5). Out of the 192 female Village Pradhans only 15 had education up to graduate level and only seven had education up to Post graduate level. The number of male members educated up to graduate and post graduate level was much higher then the females. As shown through this table the educational status of the representatives of the primary Panchayati Raj Institution can not be said to be adequate. Due to this shortcoming the cases of Pradhan Patis becoming the real power broker are still found as the lack of proper or low level of education hampers women's decision making capacity, working capability and general awareness about the various issues. Such woman were found to be holding position as proxy of their husbands and as their workload also remains unchanged therefore they do not show much interest in conducting their responsibilities or their rights and duties.

In the sample population also it was found that the educated women in all groups were knowledgeable and interested in their work, but unfortunately the level of awareness about their rights and duties among them was also not satisfactory. The 7.66 percent women who were highly educated in the 18-40 years of age group were found to be more aware about the political, social, economic and environmental issues than women above the 40 years of age group. Nearly 38 percent women in this age group were aware of the socio, political, economic and environmental issues but in the 40 and above age group the level of awareness was just 30 percent. In the 18-40 age group it was also seen that despite being highly educated some women were not well informed about the various issues whether political or others because of the lack of access to information and interest. Some of the educated respondents also opined that the knowledge about the social and political issues would not help them in their daily activities so it was not desirable to waste their time on such issues. Even the women who had been employed as teachers in the basic schools were ignorant about the current affairs etc. because of the lack of time due to their dual responsibility in home as well as in school. It was also clearly found that the men do not provide a helping hand to them in any of the domestic work because of their mindset and traditions. But it was also found the number of female teachers teaching in the primary schools has grown in the schools within the last 10 years which shows that the women have been able to take advantage of some of the new economic opportunities near their homes. Some of the respondents also told that they had also taken advantage of the National Rural

Employment Guarantee Scheme which aims to provide employment for the people in village for hundred days @ Rs.60 per day.

In view of the findings it can be said that education has increased women's status and respect in the family and they have also been supervising the education of their children but due to the general atmosphere and traditions they still have a tendency and mindset to consider themselves as an inferior to men in all regards. Such propensity among the women is the result of the historical domination of the society by men where women are still considered inferior to them therefore, despite earning almost equally their burden and work is still the same. Though the women living closer to the road head and urban towns were found to be more knowledgeable about important social and political issues, fully aware of the problems and situations and using their education in much better way than the women living in inaccessible and far away areas because of the easy accessibility of sources of information but some of them also lacked self- esteem and confidence because of their mindset of considering them inferior or less knowledgeable than men.

This is also surprising that though the women were found to be ignorant and in some cases they were not interested to claim their rights or participation in the political process but as far as the participation in the Uttarakhand movement was concerned most of respondents' reply even in the 40 and above age group was identical that they participated for securing the future of their children. However, after the creation of Uttarakhand they were not satisfied with the working of the political parties because they felt that the benefits of development were not reaching to the remote hill areas. A large number of areas were found to be lagging behind in terms of the basic facilities like good schools, water, electricity, health facilities and supply of cooking gas in time. The people, particularly the women of these areas were still cut from the main stream therefore, many of them questioned that what was the gain of the Uttarakhand state for them when neither their work load was reduced nor their standard of living improved?

It was also found in the survey that due to the high work burden only a few women in these villages were found to be active in the social, political and community affairs. Only 13.33 percent women in village Bazwar were found to be interested in the activities of the Gram Panchayats and 86.67 percent women were found to be inactive in Chepdo and in other villages also the number of women who were active in the Gram Panchayats, activities related to Mahila Mangal Dal, Gram Pȧnchayats, environmental protection etc was found to be less because of the paucity of time and their other engagements in domestic work and agriculture. But women also informed that they plant trees whenever a marriage of a daughter takes place in the family which is known as Maite Movement and they have also participated in the anti liquor agitations and organised Dharans for forcing the officials to resolve the water problem in their village level. Some women also informed that their husbands did not allow them to attend the meetings of the Gram Panchyats or Mahila Mangal Dal as usually the male members or head of the household attended these meetings. However majority of the women were in favour of more participation in the meetings of these bodies provided that their work load is reduced. They opined that the increased participation of the women would allow the solution of the problem in a more objective and practical manner.

Women's lack of interest in political affairs was exhibited when we found that 74.47 percent women were not aware of the name of the member of parliament of their constituency. Only 40 percent women said that they voted for a particular party or candidate on their own. 21.56 percent said they followed their husbands or other male members' directions. 60 percent women did not know any thing about the political rallies or party meetings generally held during the elections. Majority of the women told that their interest towards the rally of a big leader was limited to taking a look at the helicopter or to see the film star or top leader of the party not their speech. But interestingly it was reported in the local dailies during the Uttarakhand assembly elections 2007 that the women of the sixty two villages of the Bhikiasan Assembly Constituency fielded a women candidate as their candidate against the candidates of the national parties like Congress and BJP. They not only raised an amount of Rs. 62000 for contesting election but also went door to door to plead her case. (Dainik Jagran, February 15, 2007) Though their candidate lost the seat but this indicates towards the contradiction of the women of this area that on the one hand they do not show any interest towards political affiliations or political parties but on the other they feel that women could be the better alternative than men in resolving their problems. The women by adopting this stand also wanted to provide signal to the men that they were not inclined to tolerate the neglect any more and their empowerment could resolve their problems.

In fact 92 percent women felt that spreading education and providing equal opportunities for jobs and equal pay for equal work could act as a source of empowerment. Women also felt that obtaining a steady source of income was a key to changing gender relations at home and outside. In fact economic independence and empowerment of the women could lead to the sharing of work load by both the genders equally because women's lack of economic independence impedes their capacity to change their material conditions and also belittles their role and importance in the family. They also felt that the village based NGO and other institutions should also work towards this goal and through training, education and dissemination of information they could be helpful in enabling them to recognize their rights and improving their social and economic status.

However this needs to be supported by a change of mindset of the women.

Conclusion

The above discussion about the problems and prospects for the empowerment of the women of this area suggests that women are playing an important role in all the fields from domestic to agriculture, from social issues like anti- liquor agitations, environmental issues like Maite movement or Chipko movement to political movement like the Uttarakhand movement. They do take interest in the issues related to the welfare or betterment of the society but their life is full of hardships. Due to the geographical factors as well as economic and social considerations they have to work for long hours which limit their resources and access to information, communication and awareness. Moreover despite their education, the mindset and attitude of the society and its women segment has not changed much. They have a tendency of belittling their contribution and always playing second fiddle due to this reason the concern towards their developmental needs and requirements is still lacking. It also shows clearly that in these villages much has to be done to improve the status of women, to change their mind set, to reduce their drudgery, to increase their self confidence and capacities. Though the Government has launched various schemes for the education and betterment of the women like free education for the girl child and Sarv Sikshsa Abhiyaan (Education for All) but in the absence of proper infrastructure, economic empowerment and proper information these remain futile because these rarely reach to the poorest among the women. It was also found that in the villages where the women were educated they had awareness about the various governmental schemes being implemented for the benefit and welfare of the people. The women village pradhans who were educated were also making a difference by their working and thinking about the welfare of the people. This calls for giving the following more attention

- Priority to education especially for the girl child

- Publicizing the schemes for rural development more seriously
- Bringing change in the mind set by improving general awareness
- Reducing their drudgery so that they can devote their time for other issues also
- Increasing their self confidence and capacities for getting benefit of the policies
- Ensuring a better participation of the women especially the women of the lower caste segments in socio-political and economic activities.
- Developing a better pattern of connection, awareness and real empowerment

Acknowledgment

I am thankful to the research scholars Dr. Brij Mohan Rawat, Shri Rakesh Singh and Shri Purosottam Nautiyal for collecting and analyzing the field data for this study.

References

Census of India, (Govt. of India) 2001.

Haq, Mahbub ul (1990): *Human Development Report of the UNDP*, 1.

Millennium development Goals (2000)

Agarwal, Bina (1994): *A Field of One's Own: Gender and Land Rights in South Asia.* Cambridge: Cambridge University Press. Also see "'Bargaining' and Gender Relations: Within and beyond the Household." Feminist Economics, 1997. 3(1): 1-51.

Sheth Shirish S. (2006) Missing female births in India. Comment. *The Lancet,* 367.9506, Jan 21, p. 185(2).

Gender Budgeting; Initiatives for Empowerment, *Yojana,* October, 2006, pp. 5-13.

Nagaraj, A Suneetha, Vasudha (2006): A Difficult Match Women's Actions and Legal Institutions in the Face of Domestic Violence. *Economic and Political Weekly*, October 14, p. 4356.

Dogra, Bharat (2001), *Daink Jagran*, Hindi Daily , Dehradun May 21.

Jayal, Niraja Gopal (2000) *Gender and Decentralization.* Unpublished manuscript, Centre for the Study of Law and Governance, Jawaharal Nehru University, New Delhi, India.

Buch , Nirmala, (2000) *From Oppression to Assertion: A Study of Panchayats and Women in M.P, Rajasthan and U.P.* New Delhi: Centre for Women's Development Studies.

Nussbaum, Martha C (2002) Sex, Laws, and Inequality: What India Can Teach the United States *Daedalus*, Vol.131.

Dainik Jagaran: Hindi Daily (Garhwal Edition) 2004, August 3, p. 3.

Dainik Jagaran: Hindi Daily (Garhwal Edition) 2007, February 15.

4

Empowering Hill Women in Rural Development through Education and Awareness

Rama Maikhuri

Women serve as the backbone of the hill societies. They represent more than 50 percent of the population living in the hills and actively participate in the social, cultural and economic activities. They are the major contributors to the labour of farming, livestock, domestic and forest resource collections/ utilization systems etc. They play a significant role in natural resource management, on which the livelihood and the very survival of hill families/communities depend. They are an enormous source of traditional knowledge related to daily life and use of bio resources around them. Unfortunately, women have been and still are excluded from production and representation in many social, political and cultural activities. Even if they are included they do not receive their due recognition. Hill women have to face more challenges due to belonging to societies that are marginalized, traditional, inhabited in remote and far flung areas and cut off from the mainstream societies. They have to confront the hardships of living in remote and far-flung areas, harsh environment, difficult steep slopes, topography and long distances which make their tasks more arduous. Besides this the increasing tendency of the male members to migrate for employment has further increased the workload of the hill women drastically. Despite playing a very important role in nurturing the family and agriculture there is a general lack of appreciation of women's role and skills in managing and looking after the responsibilities of their own families. Due to such apathy they are often left out from the various capacity building programmes and training in rural development and decision making processes and their perspectives, needs, knowledge and contribution are also ignored.

In view of this it is being felt that there is an immediate need to provide detailed information about rural development programmes/activities (being executed by the state/central governments and their line departments) to the rural women and also empower them through education and awareness programmes. To achieve this goal education needs to be encouraged as a means of empowering women from grass root level and awareness programmes for women should also incorporate capacity building and skill developmental activities for rural development, training for formal decision making processes, leadership and strategic planning, confidence building and role in decision-making in local level governance etc. Policies that support mainstream gender issues and acknowledge women's capacity in managing their families, their resources and environment required to be formulated. Thus, hill women need to be involved in various programmes and activities necessary for improving their capacities and addressing the issues relevant to rural development as well as policy making at local, regional and national level and given equal opportunities to participate in decision making and selection of appropriate programmes/activities for rural development.

Problem, Definition and Concept of Women Empowerment

Women and their problems have acquired a steadily growing importance in our socio-cultural milieu. However even today no where in the world women enjoy equal rights and status as men. Women have always made a very significant contribution to their societies, but a patriarchal conspiracy always prevents its acknowledgement or recognition (Maria, 1980). As the creation of written historical records and the production of authoritative self-knowledge have also been controlled by men therefore appreciation of women's role in society building is also deliberately ignored. From the 1990s women empowerment has emerged as an important slogan which is gradually being integrated with participation, advocated by many scholars in the late 1970s and 1980s. But participation as a key to development was found to be highly misleading because the invisible women of earlier times were suddenly perceived as working women, and thus considered already participating in their own way in development (Thapliyal et al., 1994).

Empowerment of the women refers to a situation in which the women can decide their own destiny and also participate as equal partners in various developmental activities designed and developed for the well being of the human beings (Thapliyal et al., 1994). Empowerment in the real sense is related to the quality of life and it does not necessarily follow with rising incomes or longer life spans. A woman may be living in the midst of material comforts in a luxuries palace, and yet be powerless in terms of self-assertion, control or autonomy over her own life. Women empowerment is therefore not so much about the percentages and statistical figures that spotlight on empowerment but about increasing autonomy that empowers women as individuals in their own right, with entitlements in terms of dignity and decision making prerogatives (Sobha, 2001). One myth that we need to address and discard at the outset is the assumption that empowerment is necessary only for rural women and not for the urban women. While it is true that in some ways the average urban woman is better off in comparison with her rural counterparts but this compartmentalization into rural simplistic powerless women and urban empowered women presumes that urban women are not in need of empowerment. This is of course manifestly incorrect because gender-linked impositions are as much a part of metropolitan women's lives as they are of rural women's lives.

Although there is no denying the fact that over the past two decades, conditions of women have improved. There have been improvement in several domains of women's activity. More and more women are entering the work force. A greater number of women are overcoming traditional barriers to realize their potentials. Yet a gap exists between men and women with respect to overall development (Padamnabhan, 2001). Although a number of explanations have been advanced to account for this gap, the most important part of this analysis serves only academic purposes. What appears to be important is to devise the strategy to bridge the gap and to implement corrective measures and strategies for women's development in the right earnest (Neeta, 2000). Several programmes/activities and strategies have been geared to political, social and economic empowerment of women. Efforts have also been made to accord greater political and economic opportunity to the women as they belong to the vulnerable and disadvantaged group. In view of the overall scenario the better approach appears to be to work more for the empowerment of women at the grass root level.

Major Issues, Concerns and Action Needed

- **Recognition of hill women's roles and services**

Hill women have enormous farming workloads than men, share additional domestic responsibilities and other jobs. Appropriate technologies to reduce the physical burden of hill women need to be designed, improved, tested, implemented and disseminated using women' s knowledge.

- **Women's education, information and communication**

  Illiteracy and lack of access to health-related information affects hill women more than men. Education need to be encouraged as a means of empowering women because educated women due to awareness and knowledge delay marriage, prefer fewer children (small family) and more likely to adopt family planning measures, and understand their rights better. A strong mechanism needs to be developed to increase grassroot women's participation and provide forum through which they can update their knowledge and advocate common interests and concerns related to the rural development. Educational and skill development programmes for women should also incorporate managerial and technical skills. Access to information about markets, other livelihoods that recognise, utilize and support the diversity of hill environment also requires to be facilitated. Capacity building activities and platforms for sharing of experiences and information with others also needs to be encouraged.

- **Livelihood versus natural resource conservation**

  Hill areas are rich in natural resources but the use of these resources purely for conservation and management purposes can lead to conflict between the resource users and authorities responsible for conservation. Banning the resource use for the local habitants may affect the marginal hill societies disproportionately, and increase the workloads for women. Such restriction on bio resources on which the inhabitants have traditional rights over centuries can also lead to rapid depletion of resources as the sense of ownership is lost by such restrictions.

- **Need for gender sensitive policies and approach**

  Although gender mainstreaming is important in developing appropriate policies in aspects of governance, women focused programmes can be useful in situations in which women lack a voice, and can help participants build confidence, social capital, and skills.

- **Training and capacity building in the area of entrepreneurship and appropriate rural technologies**

Enabling women's access to hill specific simple rural technologies would be helpful in making more productive, useful technologies as well as in providing opportunities (institutional, financial, social, micro-credit, skill etc.) to the women to use these technologies for entrepreneurships. Building women's capacities/skills does not mean just bringing new rural technologies to their doorsteps, but also addressing their organisational capacities and opening new channels of information and knowledge for the rural women. This is particularly important in the hills where women have very limited access to modern facilities or to external help for solving the local problems. Women need to be provided access to the knowledge and skills required to plan, operate and manage an enterprise so that they can sustain their enterprises with the returns. The training must focus on the conditions and resources available in the regions and help promote skills, quality management, and business development, market linkages for the products that acknowledge the cultural and biological diversities of the communities.

- **Women's involvement in advocacy and decision making bodies**

Women have an important role to play in the development of sustainable and environmentally sound production and consumption systems, but they always remain sidelined when it comes to decision making. Women's representation need to be ensured in decision making bodies at all levels. Women have to be informed about their rights and involved in decision making and development of the plans for rural progress. There is also a strong requirement of training the women in the intricacies of the policy making so that they can overcome the fear of participating in the decision making process. To bring women's issues to the fore front hill women's association should be supported and facilitated. They must be given a voice and their specific concerns need to be addressed when formulating policy initiatives and partnership.

- **Create Awareness about current development programmes for betterment of rural women**

Women and their problems have acquired a steadily growing importance in our social milieu but still serious efforts to provide them an equal or big share in development process and planning is found to be absent. For empowering women and also for their well being government have launched several developmental schemes/programmes. The major focus of all these programmes is to bring them into the mainstream of development. The special programmes have been envisaged with the view to enhance the socio-economic conditions of women in the paid employment. But unfortunately the majority of the women in rural areas are found to be unaware about these programmes/activities. Therefore, attempts for motivating and mobilizing them for participation in such activities and helping them to enjoy the fruits of their labour can only define the holistic human perspective of a community. The following need to be done to improve the scenario in the remote rural hill areas

- Training-cum-employment-cum-production centres (TEPC)
- Support to training and employment programme for women (STEP)
- Women' development cooperation
- Information systems for women
- Training package for women' development

The information about the following also needs to be given a wide publicity so that women could get maximum benefit of these schemes.

- National Commission for Women (NCW)
- Rastriya Mahila Kosh and other related schemes.
- Mahila Samriddi Yojana

In addition to this, rural women also need to be made fully aware of the other rural development programmes supported by central/state governments in the following sectors: (a) agriculture, irrigation and water management, (b) social forestry and forestry, (c) small scale village and cottage industries, (d) rural housing, (e) drinking water, (f) rural road network, (g) rural electrification and non-conventional energy sources, (h) poverty alleviation, (i) education, (j) cultural activities, health, family welfare and sanitation, (k) women and child development, social welfare, (l) social welfare of weaker sections/SC/ST/youth (m) public distribution system, and (n) Panchayati Raj, etc.

Effective participation in local level governance

The hill regions require basic structure and support systems to bring about fair, transparent and good governance. Governance is a process that includes formal government but also embraces a wider notion of all those agencies and stakeholders that play a role in the control of individuals and groups in society. Unfortunately this is totally lacking in most of the regions. For spreading the message of good governance the women at grass root level should be empowered in real sense of the term and their capacities also need to be developed. The social and political frameworks to be developed to encourage initiatives by local communities.

Conclusion

Women have always played a key role in managing and operating most of the household and agriculture activities in the rural areas of the hills. Their activities have also been helpful in maintaining the essential linkages between the forest, livestock and agriculture. Therefore, the role of women merits special recognition and consideration in development. In recent years, however, environmental degradation, poor resource management, and increased migration of men to plains have deteriorated food security and added workload of women.

Women are much more inclined than men to attend educative and training courses. After having been isolated from the development and communication for centuries, they are more curious than their male counterparts, more generous and more open to new ideas. The gap between knowledge and action, between information and implementation has widened. In order to address the issues relevant to hill women, it is necessary to improve the status of women and to strengthen women's roles in integrated rural development. Thus relevant information in various areas such as proper education, training and skill development in rural development programmes/activities facilitation, information and opportunities need to be made available or provided to rural women. Any social or developmental policy for the hills can only succeed if the needs and desires of the hill women are taken care off, under estimation or apathy towards their needs would be disastrous.

Key recommendations

- Hill women are highly knowledgeable, but lack power and resources. Their knowledge need to be considered as a valuable resource to develop new technologies and provide a stake to them.

- Out-migration of men from hills has affected women severely and has contributed to the feminization of hill agriculture – rural development. The need for gender sensitive approach which includes the participation of men to walk together has to be considered.

- Women work in a clockwise position for 16 to 18 hours a day but even then the men control the economy of the household, women should be given their due.

- Promote a rights-based approach to development and strengthen economic and technological opportunities to empower women.

- Increase access to information about market of agro-produce, appropriate rural technologies and other livelihood opportunities that utilize and conserve the diversity of bio resources.

- Promote training programmes and social services to meet the development needs

- Encourage equitable representation and participation of hill women in decision making bodies at all levels and promote them in negotiation and decision making process, including in conflicts resolution in natural resource utilization and management. Representation and participation of women in local level governance is significant to the improvement and integration of women in hill regions

- Empowerment of women in social, legal and even psychological areas is crucial for raising the standards of hill women. A regional network of women, participation in decision making, natural resource management can create an inclusive space.

References

Thapliyal, B.K., Sastry, B.K., Slater, R.R., (1994). *Economic Development of Rural Women*. NIRD, Rajendra Nagar, Hyderabad, p. 23.

Padamnabhan, B.S., (2001). Women Empowerment in Farm Sector. *Yojana*, January 2001, 45(1).

Mies Maria, (1980). *Indian Women and Patriarchy*. Concept Publishing Company, New Delhi.

Thpan, Neeta, (2000). *Need for Women Empowerment*. Rawat Publication, Jaipur.

Sobha, I., (2001). Women in Agriculture: A Case Study. *Yojana,* July 2001, 45.

5

Female Foeticide and Status of Girl Child: Theme: Awareness, Problems and Solutions

Archana Shah and Mani Kant Shah

Earlier, differential treatment of children began only *after* birth. Today this is happening even *before* birth in the mother's womb. There is growing evidence of a new form of gender discrimination that has begun earlier than before, i.e. from post natal to prenatal. Female foeticide which is yet another form of violence against females is increasingly becoming widespread. As a result, the number of girls taking birth in proportion to boys is growing lesser over the years. Sex ratio is an important demographic indicator that signifies the status of women in a community. However, the sex ratio of children in the 0 – 6 years age group is a more revealing indicator of the status of the girl child (future women). The present paper draws attention to the consistent and disturbing trend in our country of declining Child Sex Ratio wherein barring just three States/UTs, thirty one have shown a sharp drop in the 2001 census. All talk of women empowerment is meaningless unless something tangible is done to arrest this trend. Uttarakhand also seems to be a member of the community of States which is guilty of committing sex-selective genocide. The present paper discusses the trends, causes and consequences of dwindling CSR with special reference to Uttarakhand.

Sex Ratio, defined as the number of females per 1000 males, is an important and useful indicator to assess relative excess or deficit of men or women in a given population at that point of time. The Child Sex Ratio (CSR) of any region is a reflection of the status of women/girl children in the community. A healthy CSR is one where there are roughly the same number of boys and girls and most societies in the industrialized world have a healthy CSR. However, in India this is apparently not so because 2001 census has shown that 31 States/UTs in India have registered a decline in CSR during 2001. A detailed look at the CSR of India for the past four decades shows that it has been declining continuously and the decline has been sharpest from 1981 onwards (Table 1).

Table 1: Child Sex Ratio, 1961 - 2001

Year	*Sex Ratio (0-6)*	*Variation (Points)*
1961	976	
1971	964	- 12
1981	962	- 2
1991	945	- 17
2001	927	- 18

Looking at the CSR of different States, as clear from Table 2, the North Western states have shown the worst decline. Alarming trends have been discerned in some states like Punjab, Himachal Pradesh, Gujarat and Delhi. Only three regions, namely Kerala, Pondicherry and Lakshwadeep have shown an increasing trend between 1991 and 2001. The magnitude of decline in CSR over two decades i.e. 1991 and 2001, of some major states and/or UTs of India namely, Punjab (-77), Haryana (-60), Himachal Pradesh (-55), Chandigarh (-54), Delhi (-47), Gujarat (-45) and Uttarakhand (-41) is abominably high. Even the UT Dadra & Nagar Haveli (-34) has shown a relatively high magnitude of decline in CSR when in 1991 it had a CSR favouring the girl child. The CSR of sixteen regions is lower than the overall sex ratio of the respective states. These are Andhra Pradesh (961 vs. 978), Chattisgarh (975 vs. 989), Goa (938 vs. 961), Gujarat (883 vs. 920), Haryana (819 vs. 861), Himachal Pradesh (896 vs 968), Karnataka (946 vs. 965), Kerala (960 vs. 1058), Maharashtra (913 vs. 922), Manipur (957 vs 978), Orissa (953 vs. 972), Pondicherry (967 vs 1001), Punjab (798 vs. 876), Rajasthan (909 vs. 921), Tamilnadu (942 vs. 987) and Uttarakhand (908 vs. 962).

Table 2: Sex Ratio of Total Population and Child Population in the Age Group 0-6 Years, 1991 and 2001

India / State / UTs	*Sex Ratio (Females per 1,000 Males)*			
	Total Population		*Child Population (0 -6 Years)*	
	1991	*2001*	*1991*	*2001*
India	*927*	*933*	*945*	*927*
States				
1. Andhra Pradesh	972	978	975	961
2. Arunachal Pradesh	859	893	982	964
3. Assam	923	935	975	965
4. Bihar	907	919	953	942
5. Chhattisgarh	985	989	984	975
6. Delhi	827	821	915	868
7. Goa	967	961	964	938
8. Gujarat	934	920	928	883
9. Haryana	865	861	879	819
10. Himachal Pradesh	976	968	951	896

(Contd.)

(Contd. Table 2)

India / State / UTs	Sex Ratio (Females per 1,000 Males) Total Population		Child Population (0-6 Years)	
	1991	2001	1991	2001
India	927	933	945	927
11. Jammu & Kashmir[1]	N.A	892	N.A	941
12. Jharkhand	922	941	979	965
13. Karnataka	960	965	960	946
14. Kerala	1,036	1058	958	960
15. Madhya Pradesh	912	919	941	932
16. Maharashtra	934	922	946	913
17. Manipur[2]	958	978	974	957
18. Meghalaya	955	972	986	973
19. Mizoram	921	935	969	964
20. Nagaland	886	900	993	964
21. Orissa	971	972	967	953
22. Punjab	882	876	875	798
23. Rajasthan	910	921	916	909
24. Sikkim	878	875	965	963
25. Tamil Nadu	974	987	948	942
26. Tripura	945	948	967	966
27. Uttar Pradesh	876	898	927	916
28. Uttaranchal	937	962	949	908
29. West Bengal	917	934	967	960
Union Territories				
1. Andaman & Nicobar Islands	818	846	973	957
2. Chandigarh	790	777	899	845
3. Dadra & Nagar Haveli	952	812	1,013	979
4. Daman & Diu	969	710	958	926
5. Lakshadweep	943	948	941	959
6. Pondicherry	979	1001	963	967

Source: Census of India 2001.

Eleven regions have a CSR which is lower than the national average (927), namely Punjab (798), Haryana (819),

Chandigarh (845), Delhi (868), Gujarat (883), Himachal Pradesh (896), Uttarakhand (908), Rajasthan (909), Uttar Pradesh (916), Maharashtra (913) and Daman & Diu (926).

Progressively low values of CSR of almost all Indian states have lead to a deficit of girls. This deficit has over the past ten years increased many times. Highest deficit of girls exists in Punjab (16.26 per cent) followed by states/UTs like Haryana (14.06 per cent), Chandigarh (11.33 per cent), Delhi (8.92 per cent) and Gujarat (7.35 per cent). The deficit of girls is fast increasing in Himachal (5.98 per cent), Uttarakhand (4.72 per cent), Rajasthan (4.62 per cent) and Maharashtra (4.2 per cent). As we can see, Uttarakhand has also shown a rise in deficit of girls from a small value of 0.42 per cent in 1991 to a figure large enough to cause worry.

Child Sex-Ratio in Uttarakhand: The Picture Within

When we examine the male-female sex-ratio in the child population (0 – 6 years) for Uttarakhand, the picture that emerges does not augur good and emanates signals of dangers lying within. Uttarakhand ranks as the seventh member in the community of states reporting low CSR. The 2001 Census shows that there are only 908 female children for every 1000 male children in the age-group of 0 – 6 years in Uttarakhand. This simply means there are about 92 missing girls for every thousand boys. As already established, there has been a significant decline in CSR over a span of ten years in Uttarakhand. The CSR has dropped a whopping 41 points from 949 in 1991 to 908 in 2001. Added to this is a worrying fact that this decline is not an isolated phenomena restricted to a couple of districts alone. On the contrary, this decline is universal to all the thirteen districts in the state. In 2001, while eleven districts recorded CSRs ranging from 902 to 953, two districts, Dehradun (894) and Haridwar (862), registered the lowest CSR in the state. A decrease of 50 points and above has been observed in three districts i.e. Pithoragarh (-62), Pauri Garhwal (-54) and Dehradun (-50).

Remaining ten districts have recorded a decline of 13 to 46 points over a decade. Moreover, as pointed out earlier, Uttarakhand is one of the members of the group of states that have a CSR which is lower than the National CSR. Again, it is also included in the group of states with a CSR value that is lower than its own general sex ratio (964). Consequently, it appears that a deficit of girls has begun to be registered in Uttarakhand too.

Reason for Declining Child Sex Ratio

Several reasons are attributed to explain the consistently low levels of CSR and its further decline in the country. Some of the important reasons commonly put forward are listed below:

- Neglect of the girl child resulting in their higher mortality at younger ages
- High maternal mortality
- Sex-selective female abortions
- Female infanticide
- Change in sex ratio at birth

Of all the explanations offered for the decline in the CSR, the most convincing one is attributed to female foeticide (Bose. A and Shiva. M, 2003). In this paper, sex selective abortions or female foeticide is discussed as a plausible reason for declining CSR in the state of Uttarakhand as well. Although there is a scarcity of information based on concrete research, news filtering from different sources suggests that the practice of female foeticide is spreading in this state too just as in some of the other north-western states. The trend towards 'masculinization' of the population seems to have begun in Uttarakhand too.

Causes of Female Foeticide

In recent times, female foeticide or sex-selective abortions made possible by technological advances in pre-natal diagnostic techniques have been the major factors responsible for the declining sex ratio. Advances in medical science have resulted in sex-determination such as sonography, fetoscopy, needling, chorion villi biopsy (CVB), amniocentesis and ultrasound. Sex-selective abortions have been greatly facilitated by the misuse of diagnostic procedures that can determine the sex of the foetus. The underlying cause for this practice is the cultural preference for sons ingrained in our Indian society. Several cultural and economic factors have made a daughter an unwanted liability and a son a much coveted asset. Adoption of small family norm and the consequent decline in fertility induces couples to control not just the number and spacing of children but also the sex-composition of their families.

During the past two decades there has been a growing alliance between tradition and technology: tradition reflected in the 'son complex' and technology reflected in aminocentesis, which was later replaced by ultrasonography (Bose. A and Shiva. M, 2003). It appears that this practice of resorting to prenatal sex-determination and opting for female foeticide is on the rise in Uttarakhand. "While in the plains, women have always suffered discrimination, women in hills traditionally enjoyed a better status. So female foeticide in hills assumes greater sociological significance," says Madhu Gurung who investigated the decline in the sex ratio and its links with female foeticide, for the Women's Feature Service with the aid of a National Foundation of India fellowship in 1998-1999 in selected states of India, including Uttaranchal (now Uttarakhand).

Uttarakhand has never had any history of female infanticide. The contribution of the girls to housework and farming was valued and they even fetched a bride price. But of late, Uttarkhand is undergoing a shift and new values seeping in from outside are slowly replacing the age-old traditional ones. Today, there seems to be a drastic change in the thinking patterns of the hill community. This is evident from the fact that a "majority of the hill women accept pre-natal sex determination tests and female foeticide as the most effective way of limiting their family". Even the illiterate masses in remotest part of the hills display an awareness of the ultrasound and are quick to associate its use with identification of sex of the unborn child rather than its actual benefit of detecting genetic disorders. Madhu Gurung pins the blame squarely on the phenomenon of "Male Migration" that has been increasing over the years. Due to limited or non-existent employment opportunities in the mountains, men migrate in search of work leaving behind their women to look after home, farmland and family. Migration has brought in new values that were once alien to the mountain society and are largely anti-woman. As more and more men from hills have been coming to the plains for employment, they have over the years picked up the same gender bias, and the preference for a son, bringing about a change in the thinking. Besides this, increasing remittances of money from outside (as a result of migration) also seems to have inflated demands for dowry, resulting in very high costs for marrying off daughters. New values as regards family size and the rise in marriage expenses for daughters together with low bargaining power for women result in smaller families and a decline in the number of female children. (Larsen.M, Gooch.P and Hatti. N, 2005). This is a four-year study that covered five states, namely Karnataka, Tamil Nadu, Himachal Pradesh, Uttar Pradesh and Uttarakhand. Its findings indicated that in Uttarakhand, differences in agrarian production appear to influence the child sex ratio. The study suggests that in places where farming is essential for the economic survival of the household, the woman's contribution to the household is considered important and her status is higher. In places like Pithoragarh where increasing remittances of money from outside as a result of migration of men folk to places outside to undertake lucrative employments, agriculture is no longer considered important for the economic survival of the family.

Migration may be having an indirect impact contributing to lowering of CSR in the state. Women are the backbone of agriculture in Uttarakhand. They perform almost all tasks associated with farming leave aside ploughing which is left to the men. Men migrate from the mountains to the plains in search of lucrative employment in the government or private sector. Many join the army and others take up menial jobs such as laborers, maids, drivers, cooks in hotels, house-hold help, guards etc. Such families rely on "money-order economy". When men are in better jobs such as the army, they are more likely to send home more money than the men who are in lesser paid and less prestigious jobs. In the case of former, the reliance of such families on agriculture is likely to decline than the other families which are more-or-less victims of poverty. The survival of latter is still largely on agriculture which is predominantly the domain of women. So for such families women will still hold value for their prospective contribution in agriculture and the consequent survival of the family. But in families where the men are doing well for themselves in other places, their dependence on agriculture is likely to weaken and as a result, women's contribution to farming will be of little concern. In such families enriched with remittances from working men in the plains, new value systems will develop as a result of outside influences. These will be reflected in their preference for limiting the size of family and in desiring sons over daughters. This means that the strength of dependence upon agriculture is directly proportional to the value of daughters. However it is important to add a note of caution here that in order to arrive at concrete conclusions, the declining trends of child-sex ratio needs to be explored further by relating it to other variables such as sex-ratio at birth, migration patterns by gender and age, food consumption patterns, and sex selective mortality indicators. Studies are also needed to explore various home based methods of child abortion in rural and urban areas if and wherever they may exist.

Impact of Declining Sex Ratio: A Glimpse into the Future

Sociologists have speculated that the worst scenario of an imbalance in sex ratio may result in creation of a womanless society. In any case, it would create social tensions when the eligible men will be unable to find women to marry. This would escalate crimes against women and lead to greater incidence of rape, sharing of women within and outside wedlock, abductions, and in general, a reduction in women's freedom and mobility. The renowned demographer Ashish Bose, known also as the generator of the term BIMARU for demographically sick states, has coined the acronym DEMARU for Daughter Eliminating Male Aspiring Rage for Ultrasound (in short Daughter Killers). Needless to say, Uttarakhand's potential inclusion in this group of DEMARU states is not a laudable achievement and nothing to be proud of. It is time that attention is paid to the cause behind the steady decline in CSR and to take corrective measures to arrest this decline by adopting measures to control female foeticide all over India.

References

Bose Ashish, *India's Unborn Daughters - Victims of Demographic Terrorism* http://www.isical.ac.in/~wemp/Papers/PaperAshishBose.doc.

Bose Ashish and Shiva Mira, (2003), *Darkness at Noon: Female Foeticide in India*, VHAI.

Census of India (2001), Provisional Population Totals, Chapter 6, Sex Composition of the Population, Series 1, India, Paper 1 of 2001,

Census of India, (2001), Series-1, India: Primary Census Abstract, Total Population: Table A-5.

Census of India, (1991), Series I- India, Part IV A – C Series: Socio Cultural Tables, Vol. I and II.

Census of India, (1981), Series I- India, Part IV A: Social and Cultural Tables, (Tables C-I to C-6).

Larsen Mattias, Gooch Pernille & Hatti Neelambar, (2005), *Uncertainty and Discrimination: Family Structure and Declining Child Sex Ratios in Rural India*, Lund Papers in Economic History, No. 99, Sweden.

Mishra Manjari, (2000), *Ultrasound Test Popular in Remotest Hill*, The Times of India News Service, 16 February http://uttarakhand.prayaga.org/news-2000-1.html#14a

6

Women Participation in Watershed Management: A Field Study of Garhwal and Shiwalik Hills

Himanshu Bourai

After the 73rd constitutional amendment watershed development has been included in the schedule of subjects to be handled by Panchyants. This provides opportunity for combining development of grassroots democracy and natural resources in symbiotic manner. A watershed is a naturally defined geographical area that drains to a common point. The concept of sustainable land management on watershed basis is quite ancient in India. The community based non-statutory institutions like tank irrigation system particularly of South India, Guhls (Water conveyance channels on contours) of Himalayas and Van Panchyats could be taken as examples of traditional knowledge and strength (J.S. Samra) about watershed management of India.

Watershed Management

To a commoner watershed is a drainage basis of a stream. Technically watershed is a hydrological entity. It is an area expansion of land from which the runoff flows through a natural drain as gullies or streams or rivers. Therefore, area of land falling on a watershed is hydrologically inter-related and it has its own natural drainage system. Unfortunately due to mismanagement of water resources more than 70 percent of the flowing water goes waste into the seas which also cause extensive flood damage in route, costing the country thousands of crores of rupees in flood damage alleviation annually. (Parthasarathy, 2000) Land degradation is also caused by both water and wind erosions at almost extreme hydrological situations of flood and drought, respectively. Hence, if wind and water erosion is controlled, land degradation could be avoided or reduced. In view of this watershed management is an integrated approach of conservation of land, water of biomass for ultimate benefit of mankind. The following data provides an idea about the quantity of the precious water resource being wasted in the absence of its proper utilization.

Total water flow through rivers, quantity used and lost by draining into sea

Total water flow through rivers in India 1869 km^3/annum

Quantity of water used at present = 550 km^3/annum (roughly 30%).

Quantity of water that goes waste into sea = 1319 km^3/ annum (roughly 70%)

Watershed is understood to be a catchment's area feeding identifying drainable system, such as a stream or river, watershed contains a number of biophysical resources: soil and water, along with vegetation in the form of trees, grasses and crops, and also provides livestock production. The idea of watershed management was adopted by multipurpose Damodar Valley development project (Chaitali Pal). A major policy change was made in 1954 in establishing a chain of soil and water conservation, research, demonstration and training centers all over India. About 42 micro-watersheds were developed since 1956 with major thrust on biophysical issues especially hydrology. Research findings of this limited experience became basis of lunching river valley projects for conserving various catchments in 1961-62. Another paradigm shift in favour of participatory and demand driven watershed management was initiated by Central Soil and Water Conservation Research and Training Institute, Dehradun during 1974 (J. S. Samra,). The concept had since been reiterated in all plan documents. A series of integrated development projects for local areas were started in early 1980, first by ICAR and later by Ministry of Rural Development, Ministry of Environment and Forests and Ministry of Planning and Programme Implementation dealing with rural area development, employment, poverty alleviation and watershed development. Any watershed development programme undertaken for a better and successful management of the water resource should focus on the following steps and conditions:

Major steps of watershed development

1. Site selection.
2. Bench mark resource survey.
3. Development of operational WSM Plan.
4. People's participation.
5. Implementation of Plan.
6. Monitoring.
7. Feed back.

Conditions of successful watershed management programme

1. The involvement of all sections of the society, including women.
2. Identification of people's priorities.

3. The use of simple but effective technology which includes;
- interventions to manage runoff water through watershed development by:

  Cheap methods, local materials and labour.

As watershed management is a holistic and sustainable development programme which includes water management, community managed erosion prevention and wide spread a forestation. Since people are the most important agents of carrying out the schemes of watershed management therefore major decisions regarding such programmes should be taken by the Gramsabha through a democratic system. This would lead to full and active participation of local people, in building up land-based resources as well as overall resource conservation. The management of watershed would improve the crop productively, standard of living and socio-economic and environmental conditions. The watershed management programme requires not only participation of the people at the village level, assessment of their problems, needs and interests but also planning at the institutional and field level. People also need to be involved at the decision making process level and told the benefits of the successful watershed management.

People's participation and watershed management

People's participation in watershed management is as vital as the scientific input in the planning and designing of the programme. Importance of people's participation in making the programme self sustainable is now widely accepted by the planners, administrators, academicians and practitioners all over the world (B.L. Dhyani). According to Banki "participation means, a dynamic process in which all member of a work group contribute, share, or are influenced by the interchange of ideas and activities towards problems solving or decision making". (Banki 1981). Watershed management also means the participation of all the farmers in all the stages of soil and water conservation programmes right from designing of various structures through monitoring and evaluation of their performance. (Singh, 1990)

Purpose of people's participation

People's participation increases awareness in the community about project, its objectives, polices and results. The plan is drafted to take care of the priorities with full involvement of farmers, indigenous knowledge and needs and is implemented with the purpose of maximum possible work in the watershed by involvement of local people. It also aims to extend modern land management technologies to the farming community to obtain their willing support in the programme and make it the integral part of their farming activities. It also intends to develop human resource base of watershed and building of the local institutions for follow up action.

Women's participation in watershed management programmes

As women are the most important component of any developmental schemes to be undertaken for village development therefore any plan which avoids women's participation cannot be successfully implemented. It is ironical that despite this fact women's participation in various schemes is still lacking and it is not as per their population. India's Gender Related Development Index (GDI) places India in the rank of 112. We may feel comfortable if compared with Pakistan (Rank 116), Bhutan (119) and Bangladesh (123). But if compared with Sri Lanka (76) and China (79) we are far below in the gender development index. One can feel happy that over the years that GDI in India is inching forward because in 1997 India's rank was 118, undoubtedly there has been some progress but this is not very significant.

Role of the Rural Women in Managing Resources

Most rural women are directly dependent on their immediate environment and their own skills in using these for their daily necessities of life (Recheluae, 1985). Women, particularly those living in the rural areas of Third World countries, play a major role in managing natural resources – soil, water, forest and energy. Their tasks in agriculture and animal husbandry as well as in the household make them the daily mangers of the living environment. They have a profound knowledge of the plants, animals and ecological process around them.

The principal victims of environmental degradation generally are the most under privileged people and the majority of these happen to be the women (Senghor, 1985). The problems of the women and those of the environmental degaradation are very much interrelated as both suffer and marginalized by existing developmental policies. Moreover because of the complex cycles of poverty, inappropriate development and environmental degradation, the poor people have been forced into ways of living which induce further destruction and environmental degradation. (Aidoo, 1985). The poor women even though they may be having the knowledge to promote sustainability have no other choice but to exploit natural resources for their survival. Women constitute about half of the world's population, they account for 75 percent of the working hours, and contribute up to 30 percent of the official labour force, yet receive only ten per cent of the income and own less than one percent of the world's property. The situation is rather appalling in the developing countries. In India, women constitute 48.5 percent of the rural population. About 75 percent of the rural women belong to the families of small and marginal farmers. Two third of them are illiterate and provide most of the farm labour by putting in 14-18 hours of productive manual labour. Growing food has been as interminable saga of her life. No field operation is beyond her competence. She is at her best in sowing, transplanting, weeding, winnowing, threshing, storing, marketing, rearing livestock and poultry. Due to her total involvement in these operations, the farm women in India are considered to be the backbone of the Indian agriculture.

Although women have never been involved directly as a 'target group' in watershed management programmes in general and soil and water conservation programme in particular, yet these programmes have changed the nature of the natural resources especially that of soil, water and vegetation and such an environmental friendly effort may also result in increased pressure on farm women. Watershed management is now a widely accepted technology for resource management in totality and coherently with people's participation in a holistic manner. Women participation in WSM is an important component of people participation in WSM.

Meaning of women participation in WSM

To understand the women's participation in WSM, to know the number of women who have come forward to take part in the preparation and planning of natural resource management and watershed management, to assess the women's satisfaction level about monetary and the environmental benefits, involvement in taking decisions on the rights of the watershed management, increase in the level of confidence to work on other developmental activities by using the experience in working on the WSM a diagnostic survey was conducted in five WSM like : Sukhomajri WSM, Relmajra WSM, Fakot WSM, Chandrabadni and Danda WSM and Chandrabhaga MSM.

Methodology of the survey

(A) Diagnostic survey was conducted on the basis of sample survey in Sukhomajri WSM, Relmajra WSM and Fakot WSM of Central soil and Water Conservation Research and Training Institute, Chandrabadni and Danda WSM of Bhuvneshwari Mahila Ashram (NGO), Chandrabhaga WSM of State Govt. of Uttar Pradesh (now in Uttarakhand).

(B) In these watersheds families were selected for survey on the basis of age group of women and land holding capacities.

(C) A total number of 297 women between the age group of 20 to 75 and holding the land between one Bigha to 20 Bigha and less were interviewed through structured questionnaires.

(D) The focus of the survey was to know how they are participating in watershed management activities directly or indirectly and how the participation of women can be increased from their point of view.

An introduction to the Watershed projects and the findings of the field work has been discussed in the following text.

1. Sukhomajri WSM

The Sukhomajri WSM project, which has been acclaimed nationally and internationally as a model is basically the contribution of the team of experts of CSWCRTI, Chandigarh and Forest Department (FD), Haryana. The concept of WSM in the context of Sukhomajri has been defined as "the integration of technologies within the boundaries of drainage system for optimum development of land, water and plant resources according to meet the minimum needs of people." (Mittal S.P. 1996). This approach according to Mittal has paved the way for integrating the existing technologies for land treatment, soil and water conservation, forestation, augmentation and development of water resources and increasing crop and animal production, to ultimately improve the socio-economic conditions of an area in holistic manner. People's participation in WSM planning and implementation is considered as vital and crucial.

Sukhomajri village

Sukhomajri is a small hamlet located at Shiwalik foothills, 30km. north-east of Chandigarh on Pinjore-Nalagarh road at 30.50' latitude and 76.53' longitude, in Panchkula district of Haryana. In 1975, the village had no resource of irrigation. The entire agricultural land 52ha was under rain fed single cropping system. Small land holdings (less than one hectare per family) and frequent crop failures made it difficult for the people to sustain themselves. In view of this each family was keeping large number of goats to eke out a living. Goats were allowed to graze freely in the nearly hills and years of over grazing have made even the toughest of shrubs and grazes scrawny. Villagers restored to illicit cutting of trees from hilly areas for fuel wood. Denudation in the surrounding hills was so fast that hill slopes once clothed with green cover were rendered totally grassless. Sheer needs of substance forced the poor villagers to decimate the very base of their survival. Today with managing its water resources Sukhomajri presents an example of participation of people for sustainable development of WSM. Since without people's participation, it is difficult to achieve the goal of 'Integrated WSM and if the goals are difficult to achieve one can understand the causes of gaps behind the concept and evolve this concept for future watershed management.

Profile of Sukhomajri Village and WSM

Total No. of families	119
Total population	720
Women population	178
Av. Family size	6.07
Literacy rate	55%

Public facilities

Primary School	1
Anganwadi	1
Dharamshala	1
Private shops	5
Temple	1

The following public facilities are required for the women on priority basis

A. Sub-health centre

E. Adult Education centre

B. Primary health centre
C. Veterinary centre
D. Secondary & High Schools
F. Co-operative Bank and
G. Rural Bank

Relmajri WSM

The project area is located in village Relmajri, district, Ropar (latitude 31^0N, longitude 76^028'E) at an elevation of 280 m above the sea level. This village is situated at the Shiwalik foothills, about 9 km. north from Ropar on Ropar-Hoshiarpur road. The watershed drains into river Satluj. There are six namely Bara Chor, Chitkar, Sukla, Badholi, Gufanwala and Khol, which carry the runoff water from six independent sub-catchments. In comparison to Sukhomajri this is a big village with heterogeneous society. In this village there are about 13 communities including S.C. and S.T. who are mostly landless and represent multiple problems being faced by of India. On the other hand in Sukhomajri there is only one community with only one caste people.

Profile of village selected under Relmajri

Status	**Number**
Total No. of village	1
Total No. of family	42
Total population	336
Women population	144
Average family size	8.0
Literacy Rate	61%

Public Facilities:

Public facilities	**Number**
Primary School	1
High School	1
Community Centre	1
Dharamshala	1

Primary Health Centre	1
Private shop	1
Temple	1
Dispensary	1
Post office	1
Punjab National Bank	1
Co-operative society	1
Milk Dairy	1

Public facilities required by the people:

Public facilities

(A) Sub health Centre
(B) Primary health Centre
(C) Veterinary Centre
(D) Adult Education Centre
(E) Rural Bank
(F) Nursery

Chadrabadni and Danda watersheds

Chadrabadni and Danda watersheds are located in the proximity of Devprayag the confluence of the Alaknanda and Bhagirathi. These watershed support 534 famililties (408 in Chandrabadni watershed and 126 famililties in Danda watershed). These families are spread over 18 villages (11 in Chandrabadni Watershed and 7 in Danda watershed).

Following activities have been undertaken in these areas during the past years under WSM.

- A forestation and slope stabilization.
- Rainwater harvesting.
- Drinking water augmentation.
- Facilitating irrigation
- Village feeder roads.
- Nursery development
- Human resource development

Besides this the following work has also been carried out in these areas

Activity	*No. of Village*
Trenching	4
Check Dam	3
Plantation	1
Retaining wall	3
Open well	2
Khal renovation	1
Tank repairing	1
Pipeline	1
Tank	1
Canal	2
Feeder road	6
Nursery	2

Profile of the villages selected (under Bhuvneshwari Mahila Ashram)

Status	*Number*
Total No. of village	18
Total No. of family	534
Total population	3000
Women population	1068
Average family size	5.62
Literacy Rate	54.83

Available Public Facilities

Public facilities	*Number*
Primary School	7
High School	-

(Contd.)

(Contd.)

Public facilities	*Number*
Health Centre/ dispensary	3
Aanganwari	4
Private shop	7
Temple	3
Post office	2

Public facilities required by the people: Road, Drinking water, Hospital, High school, Co-operative bank, Rural Bank and Veterinary Hospital.

Chandrabhaga watershed

Chandrabhaga micro-watershed of Risikesh Division is situated between 78^{0}142 353 to 78^{0}192 483 E and 30^{0}072 163 N, 30^{0}152 163 Chandrabhaga micro-watershed is in Tehri-Garhwal district. Talani village of this watershed is situated in Narendra Nagar Tehsil of Tehri district 15 km from Rishikesh on Rishkesh-Tehri road. It was selected purposively because women participation in village level activities was high in comparison to other villages of Garhwal region.

Profile of village selected under Chandrabhaga Watershed

Status	*Number*
Total No. of families	48
Total Population	261
Women population	64
Average family size	5.4
Literacy Rate	70.73

Available Public Facilities

Public facilities	**Number**
Primary and secondary school	1

Public facilities required by the people: Road connectivity for the village, Sub-health Centre, Aganwari and Veterinary Hospital

Fakot watershed

Fakot watershed is situated in the middle Garhwal region which represents Western Himalayas. The watershed is situated between 78^0202 to 78^0222 E and 20^0132 to 20^0152 N with folded sedimentary rocks (Shale and stale). Fakot watershed is in Tehri Gahrwal district 50 km from Rishikesh on Rishikesh- Tehri highway. It was selected purposively as it has maximum severely degraded area (32.31) of the Garhwal region. The district represents ecological fragility, marginality, poor resource conditions, high risk and low pay farming situation. It is a typical watershed representing reserve forests, civil soyam, private and common property land uses and severe soil erosion problems. The watershed drains into river Hiyul which is a tributary of major system of Uttarakhand hills i.e. the river Ganga. The important point considered in the selection of watershed was its demonstration value. The watershed is situated on Rishikesh -Tehri highway which is the only important highway to connect the two districts namely Tehri and Uttrakashi, where maximum soil erosion problem exists. Pre-existence of Community Development Block near the watershed which provided necessary infrastructural facilities was another favourable point in selection of this watershed programme.

Profile of the village Fakot

Status	*Number*
Total No. of village	1
Total No. of family	153
Total population	965
Women population	385
Average family size	7.8
Literacy Race	68.7%

Public facilities

Public facilities	*Number*
Primary School	1
Block development office	1
High School	1
Cooperative society	1
Health Centre	1
V. Hospital	1
Aaganwari	1
Inter College	1
Private shop	6
Fair prices shop	1
Temple	1
Block Dev. Centre	1
Horticulture Department.	1
Medical store	2

Public facilities required: Road (within the village), Drinking water, Seed Bank, Compost pit and Water storage tank

Result and discussion

Table 1: Profile of Watersheds

Watershed	*Sukhomajri*	*Rel Majra*	*Chandra-badni danda*	*Chandra-bhaga*	*Fakot*
Year of starting the project	I 1975, II 1978 III 1980, IV 1985	1992	1998	1994	1974

(Contd.)

(Contd. Table 1)

Watershed	*Sukhomajri*	*Rel Majra*	*Chandra-badni danda*	*Chandra-bhaga*	*Fakot*
Catchement area (ha)	4.3 9.2 1.5 2.6	59	-	-	15
Command area (ha)	6.0 20.0 2.0 5.0	21.88	7356 (map area) 3440	-	-
Storage capacity (m³)	8000 55600 9500 19300	13.7	-	-	-
Total investment in Rs.	72000 109000 23000 150000	2913230	-	-	50000
Year of the withdrawal of the project	1981 - -	-	-	1997	-
Project Name continued	-	-	Continued	-	-

Literacy and watershed management

Literacy and Education are reasonably good indicators of development in a society and as watershed programme are one of the most important development programmes, therefore, there is a close relation between literacy and WSM. But as it is a well known fact that without food security there cannot be any literacy, therefore, it was found that these WS has been able to give food security to the people and they have started thinking about education. As far as the women are concerned it was found that though in every WS the literacy rate of the people has increased yet there is still an urgent need to provide

Table 2: Educational Status of Women before and after WS Project (%)

Educational Level	*WATERSHED*									
	Sukho-majri		*Relmajra*		*Chandrabadni danda*		*Chandrabhaga*		*Fakot*	
	B.P.	*A.P.*	*B.P.*	*A.P.*	*B.P.*	*A.P.*	*B.P.*	*A.P.*	*B.P.*	*A.P.*
Literate	0	55	1.59	61.36	54.50	54.83	51.56	70.73	10.41	68.7
Illiterate	100	45	98.41	38.37	45.49	45.16	48.43	29.26	89.58	31.2

(B.P. before project, A.P. after project)

education to all the women. In every watershed women also opined that their participation can increase only after getting good education. They clearly felt that because of illiteracy or just being literate it was not possible for them to participate at all the levels of the developmental schemes.

As shown in Table- 2 the literacy rate has increased in all the watersheds after the project because food security and overall socio-economic development has been achieved. It was also found that every girl child is going to school which can be taken as an important achievement.

Table 3: Literacy Rate according to 2001 Census (%)

National and State wise	*Total*	*Male*	*Female*
India	65.38	75.85	54.16
Punjab	69.95	75.63	63.55
Hariyana	68.59	79.25	56.31
Uttaranchal	72.28	84.01	60.26

In comparison to India and its states, literacy rate of watershed as shown in the Table- 2 in rural areas is high.

Problems: However higher education is still a problem for girls and mostly girls could not continue their education after 5th or 8th class in village. This shows that even today parents are not ready to send their daughters outside the village for their education. They think that job opportunities are very low and after getting education the girls would not work in fields. Due to this reason they think that the educated girls create a new type of social problem in the village.

LAND

Since women are at the center of world food production producing more than 80 percent of the food in some countries therefore, any analysis of land resources must include an appreciation of their central role. Land is the foundation on which life depends and if land is healthy then agriculture and pasturage will yield food in plenty otherwise the ecosystem will show signs of strains and food production will become more difficult. Even with the initiation of agrarian reforms, the politics of land ownership ensures that the most productive land remains in the hands of a few.

Table 4: Family wise land holding (%) in different watersheds

Land Distribution (in Hac.)	*Water Shed*				
	Sukho-majri	*Rel Majra*	*Chandrabadni Danda*	*Chandra Bhaga*	*Fakot Watershed*
Land Less	3.44	0	2.32	0	0
0-0.5	65.51	16	69.76	81.81	31.58
0.5-1.0	17.24	12	23.25	18.18	31.58
1.0-1.5	6.89	24	4.65	-	10.52
1.5-2.0	6.89	16	0	-	26.32
More than 2.0	0	32	0	-	0

As the above table shows mostly the farmers are holding between .5 to 1 (ha) land. In Relmajra and in Sukhomajri land holding is high in comparison to Chandrabadni Danda, Chandrabhaga and Fakot watershed. The big land holdings have ensured the food security through two corps and irrigation.

However the major problems being confronted in this is the division of land within the family and only prominent people of village are getting water from dam. Other problems are mainly related to Chandrabadni and Fakot watersheds as described by the women like: (1) Scattered and limited land holding (2) low productivity as terraced farming is the only option (3) lace of technical know-how and absence of local farm related research (4) absence of means of transportation (5) Poor marketing

Table 5: Position of Land (ha)

Land	*WATERSHED*									
	Sukhomajri		*Rel Majra*		*Chandrabadni Danda*		*Chandrabhaga*		*Fakot*	
	B. P.	A.P.	B. P.	A.P.	B. P.	A.P.	B. P.	A.P.	B. P.	A.P.
Irrigated Land	-	98.83%	40.85%	71.07%	15.97%	15.97%	77.89%	77.89%	11.84%	25.60%
Un irrigated Land	100%	1.15%	59.15%	28.92%	84.02%	84.2%	22.10%	22.10%	88.16%	74.40%

avenues and poor finance. (6) Shortfall of labour due to migration. (7) No storage facilities.

In the opinion of the women of Garhwal Himalayas the following practices would be able to bring an improvement in the situation:

- Chakbandi and Mukhalsar practices to be established.
- Rain water harvesting/ storage be made mandatory
- Mixed plantation to be taken up in van panchayats.
- Storage facilities to be extended in important centers.
- Information dissemination about modern farming techniques and high yield variety of seeds to the farmers.
- Traditional forming with modern inputs to be taken up at a large scale.
- Improvement in transportation facilities.
- Bio fencing with local varieties of Rambans to ward of wild animals.

As shown in the Table-5 the dam irrigated land has increased in Sukhomajri, Relmajra and Fakot watersheds but as Chandrabadni danda is in initial stage and there is no scope for increase in land for Chandrabhaga watershed. Irrigation facilities have clearly seen through the Guhal system now converted it into cemented Guhal.

The survey findings revealed that the household related work, fodder and fuel collection work of the farm women was reducing but the agriculture work was increasing. In SM and RM watershed rest time of the women has increased but the women of Garhwal Himalaya has been working more in comparison to the women of the Shiwalik hills. Being predominantly agricultural community majority of the population in Shiwalik and Garhwal Himalayas is engaged in agriculture and associated agro based cottage industry. The lesser and often outdated technological inputs virtually compel

Table 6: Time Utilization by farm women in a day (Hours)

Activities	*WATERSHED*									
	Sukhomajri		*Rel Majra*		*Chandrabadni Danda*		*Chandra Bhaga*		*Fakot*	
	B.P.	*A.P.*	*B.P.*	*A.P.*	*B.P.*	*A.P.*	*B.P.*	*A.P.*	*B.P.*	*A.P.*
House hold including childcare	6.20	5.10	6.15	6.00	5.00	5.00	5.00	5.00	5.30	5.30
Agriculture/ Horticulture	1.10	2.10	1.15	2.00	2.40	2.20	3.00	3.30	2.45	3.45
Livestock	2.10	2.30	2.00	2.30	2.30	2.30	2.30	3.00	2.15	2.30
Fodder collection	1.10	0.30	1.30	0.30	2.30	2.30	2.30	1.00	2.30	1.00
Fuel collection	2.30	0.30	2.30	0.30	2.00	2.00	2.00	1.00	2.00	1.00
Fetching water	2.10	1.10	2.00	2.00	1.30	1.30	1.00	0.30	1.30	1.00
Entertainment	0.30	1.00	0.30	1.00	0.30	0.30	1.00	2.00	0.30	1.15
Rest	8.00	11.00	8.00	9.30	7.20	7.40	7.00	8.00	7.00	8.00

every member of family to participate in the process of production. Female members, traditionally contribute more in this regard. Since agriculture is the mainstay of hill people, the women are supposed to be deeply involved in all stages – preparing the fields, sowing, reaping, harvesting, and threshing to transporting and storing the grain. Further they have to look after the cattle and carry head loads of fodder, fuel, manure, flour and rock and clay in case of household construction work. During harvest time they often have to work after the evening meal and at times keep on working till late night. In villages where potable water, fodder or fuel is not available in closer vicinity, the women folk have to cover long distance to fetch the same. In such cases, their day begins even before dawn. The women belonging to poorer families have also to work on the agricultural field of the better-off so as to earn bread and butter for the family. The activities of weaving, knitting and stitching for routine household needs and at times for economic reasons further tax their remaining free time, if any. Thus rural women folks may have to work for almost 14 to 16 hours daily most of which, paradoxically, goes unaccounted and even unnoticed and naturally unappreciated.

Agriculture

Although rural women have contributed a lot in the growth of agriculture in India through various development programmes, yet these very programmes have stimulated their marginalization (Shiva, 1995; Mencher and Sardomoni 1982; Mics et.al, 1983 Swarup and Rajpur, 1995). The reasons are manifold such as biological, cultural, mechanical, psychological/ mythological and administrative. The relationship between women and men and environment is structured by gender-differentiated roles, rights and responsibilities with respect to the use, management and ownership of natural resources. Without understanding this mechanism even environmental friendly efforts can result in increased pressure/exploitation of

Table- 7: Time utilization of Farm women in Agriculture in a day (min)

Activities	*WATERSHED*									
	Sukhomajri		*Rel Majra*		*Chandrabadni Danda*		*Chandra-bhaga*		*Fakot*	
	B. P.	*A.P.*	*B. P.*	*A.P.*	*B. P.*	*A.P.*	*B. P.*	*A.P.*	*B. P.*	*A.P.*
Culture operator	10	20	10	20	25	25	25	35	20	35
Irrigation	0	0	0	0	30	10	40	20	10	5
Sowing/ploughing	15	20	20	25	15	15	20	20	25	35
Transplantation	15	25	10	15	15	15	10	15	20	30
Fertilizer	5	10	5	10	20	20	15	20	25	30
Weeding/Harvesting	10	20	10	20	15	15	20	25	15	15
Bunding/Threshing	5	10	10	15	30	30	30	45	25	35
Transport	10	25	10	15	10	10	20	30	25	40
Marketing	-	-	-	-	-	-	-	-	-	-

the farm women. Since, it is women's activities that protect and conserve nature's boundary in forests and agriculture in hilly ecosystem and through such conservation works she sustains human life by ensuring the availability of food, fodder and water for drinking and irrigation. Women's agricultural work in the Himalayas is largely done in the forest and other natural resources, yet it is discounted both in forestry and agriculture. (Bandhyopadhyay and Moench; 1985, Bhatti and Singh; 1987, Kaur, 1991) Even though women play a predominant role in agriculture and bear a disproportionately higher burden of farm production, they have been almost completely marginalized from extension services, training and access to productive resources. More importantly however, it is the disproportionately low percentage of women workers in the agriculture extension system that prevents it from reaching women. This male dominated extension system tends to overlook women's role in agriculture and proves ineffective in providing technical information to the women farmer. The female labour participation in agriculture in the villages includes sowing, inter-culture, harvesting, threshing, and winnowing and post harvest operations. It was interesting to observe that after the project the percentage contribution of farm women increased in agricultural activities. In Sukhomajri, Rel Majra and to some extent in Fakot and Chandrabhaga watershed multiple cropping systems have been adopted due to the facility of supplemental irrigation.

The above table shows that the overall agriculture work has incresed (-). But in the Garhwal Himalayas cemented Guhl system has decreased the work load of women (+). Now, women are spending less time in irrigation activities.

Livestock

Livestock in India plays a multiple role in the village economy by providing products for consumption and sale such as milk products, meat and wood, providing energy for agricultural activities as well for cooking and manorial inputs for croplands. In fact, it is livestock that provides some degree of stability to the village economy during periods of drought. Shiva (1988) estimates that more than two thirds of the power requirements of Indian villages are met by about 80 million work animals. She further estimates that of the 700 million tones of manure exerted by Indian cattle every year, half is used as fuel (which would otherwise require 68 million tones of wood or 27 million tones of Kerosene) and the other half as fertilizer, with dung providing 38 percent by weight and 17 percent by energy value of applied plant nutrients in India in 1975 (World Bank 1991). The scarcity of resources such as wood and Kerosene further emphasizes the crucial role played by livestock in the village economy. As started earlier, women play a predominant role in livestock management and dairy production. They fetch for the livestock, feed and/ or graze them, clean cattle sheds, collect and process dung and milk. Dung is also composted and carried out to the fields by women. In deforested parts of the country where trees and other sources of cooking fuel are scarce, women prepare cooking fuel by mixing dung with twigs and crop residues. Like most other activities, women's role in livestock management varies across the class. Women of landless and small-peasant household perform all the activities just listed above. Whereas women of medium farmer households perform tasks confined to the house, such as feeding and milking. Outside jobs in such households are carried out by hired labour. Women of rich farmer households, on the other hand, perform mainly supervisory functions. It needs to be pointed out that women's role in animal husbandry is significant because of their traditional role in integrating agriculture with animal husbandry.

It was found that work related to grazing has reduced but with the growing size of the live stock like buffaloes the milk production is increasing, as one family is holding 5 to 7 cattle (Sukhomajri and Relmajra) however the grass problem was

Table - 8: Time utilization of farm women in livestock rearing activities in a day (min)

Activities	*WATERSHED*									
	Sukhomajri		*Rel Majra*		*Chandrabadni Danda*		*Chandra Bhaga*		*Fakot*	
	B.P.	*A.P.*	*B.P.*	*A.P.*	*B.P.*	*A.P.*	*B.P.*	*A.P.*	*B.P.*	*A.P.*
Grazing	60	20	45	20	45	45	45	20	40	15
Chaffing of fodder	15	25	20	25	15	15	20	30	20	25
Cleaning the animal & Cattle sheds	10	15	10	20	30	30	20	30	25	30
Milking	15	30	15	30	20	20	20	35	15	25
Preparation of dung cake/dung related	15	30	20	30	25	25	25	35	20	30
Marketing of Milk	15	30	10	25	15	15	20	30	15	25

increasing. In comparison to Shiwalik region the animal resource has not been fully tapped in Uttarakhand. As a result the farmers have to contend with the diminishing quality of produce from the domesticated animals. The problems being faced are: (1) poor quality of stock resulting from inbreeding (2) absence of technical know- how. (3) Poor quality of fodder (4) cross breeding for better varieties rarely carried (cross breed between local variety and Jersey cow) (5) facility of veterinary hospitals missing in village.

Fuel

In many countries, forest forms the basis of civilization, and forest based settlements produced the best scientific research and cultural writings. For centuries women have gathered forest products. "The time spent in forests, gathering wood, has taught women the many uses of trees, including providing fibers for cloth, mat-making and basketry. For women, trees and forests are multifunctional. Trees offer "fuel, food and fodder"- the three 'F's as women say. With so much pressure on the land, women have little choice but to use forests. As there are no alternatives and women are required to gather wood and other biomass for fuel from wherever they can but the women rarely collect trees, they take only twigs and small branches. Unfortunately women's participation in the forestry sector is constrained in many ways: competition for land problems. land tenure; lack of time left after domestic duties; cultural taboos and lack of familiarity with forestry. Moreover, women do not have institutional and organizational support; absence of legal entitlement to land, and the low priority given to a forestation have hindered tree planting efforts. If the poor people and women are to be benefited from social forestry projects, they must be involved and have a share in the results of the projects. The need of the time is to introduce the appropriate hill and household technology to reduce women's daily drudgery. The women themselves must be involved in

Table 9: Women and Fuel Collection

Factor	*WATERSHED*									
	Sukhomajri		*Rel Majra*		*Chandrabadni Danda*		*Chandrabhaga*		*Fakot*	
	B. P.	*A.P.*	*B. P.*	*A.P.*	*B. P.*	*A.P.*	*B. P.*	*A.P.*	*B. P.*	*A.P.*
Fuel consumption/day/family	5-7kg	1-2kg	6-7kg	2-3kg	8-10kg	8-10kg	9-10kg	3-4kg	9-10kg	5-6kg
Frequency of women for collecting the fuel from forest (%)										
Every day	100*	20*	92.06*	-	93.02%	93.02%	90.75%	25%	90%	45%
Once a Week	-	-	-	25**	-	-	-	-	-	-
Twice a Week	-	80*	7.94**	75**	6.97%	6.97%	9.25%	75%	10%	55%
Once a Month	-	-	-	-	-	-	-	-	-	-
Distance covered by No. of women for collecting Fuel from forest (%) Less than 2km.	-	80*	-	75**	-	-	-	100*	-	79.16%
2 to 4km.	50*	20*	-	25**	-	-	-	-	87.5%	20.84%
4 to 6km.	30*	-	84.12**	-	53.48%	53.48%	75%	-	12.5%	-
6km.	20*	-	15.87%	-	46.51%	46.51	25%	-	-	-

* Only for men ** Men and women both.

appropriate hill and household technology to reduce women's daily drudgery. The women themselves must be involved in such innovations because they have valuable suggestions and solutions to offer.

It was found that the fuel wood consumption was decreasing because 25 percent dung was being utilized for dung-cake and also due to the use of LPG, Kerosene oil. But in the winters the wood consumption was increasing. It was suggested that through Gobergas plant, wood consumption can be reduced and the time for preparing dung cake can also be saved. It was also found that in Sukhomajri and Relmajra mostly men go for fuel collection but in Chandrabadni danda, Chandrabhaga and Fakot watershed only women go for fuel wood collection.

Fodder

The availability of fodder for the animals is a primary concern in the livestock sector. In 1985, only about 57 percent of dry fodder and 27 percent of green fodder requirements were being met (Chambers et al. 1989). Fodder has traditionally been available from different sources in different forms. In addition to permanent grazing lands, livestock grazes on government forest lands, village common land, uncultivable wastelands and fallow lands. Due to shortage of green fodder, crop residues such as rice and wheat straw make up a significant proportion of animal feed. Grazing on private lands after harvesting has also been common for under growth and crop residues. Additionally, a small proportion of livestock are fed on fodder crops that are cultivated on private lands. Since it is women who are responsible for feeding and maintaining livestock, the task of collecting fodder is undertaken primarily by them. In addition to common lands, women get fodder from landlords in exchange for labour or collect grass and residues from their fallow lands and other public lands.

Table 10: Women & Fodder Collection

Factor	*WATERSHED*									
	Sukhomajri		*Rel Majra*		*Chandrabadni Danda*		*Chandrabhaga*		*Fakot*	
	B. P.	*A.P.*	*B. P.*	*A.P.*	*B. P.*	*A.P.*	*B. P.*	*A.P.*	*B. P.*	*A.P.*
Fodder consumption/day/family	10-20kg	40-60kg	10-20kg	40-60kg	8-10kg	8-10kg	1-10kg	14-16kg	8-10kg	12-14kg
Frequency of women for collecting the fodder from forest (%)Every day	100*	30*	93**	25**	93.02%	93.02%	90.75%	20%	72.91%	62.5%
Once a Week	-	-	-	-	-	-	-	-	-	-
Twice a Week	-	75*	7.00**	75**	6.97%	6.97%	9.25%	80%	27.08%	37.5%
Once a Month	-	-	-	-	-	-	-	-	-	-
Distance covered by No. of women for collecting Fuel from forest (%)	-	80*	-	31.75**	-	-	-	80%	-	79.16%
Less than 2km.										
2 to 4km.	50*	20*	79.36%	38.25%	-	-	-	20%	87.5%	20.84%
4 to 6km.	30*	-	20.63**	-	53.48%	53.48%	75%	-	12.5%	-
6km.	20*	-	-	-	46.51%	46.51%	25%	-	-	-

* Only Men **Men and Women Equally

Table 11: Women participation in WSM planning, management and monitoring

Activities	*Women in response about activities (%)*				
	Sukhomajri	*Rel Majra*	*Chandrabadni danda*	*Chandrabhaga*	*Fakot*
Talking to village women					
at the time of planning	17.40%	42.85%	23.25%	18.75%	12%
Occasionally	-	11.11%	39.53%	56.25%	-
Frequently	82.85%	46.03%	37.20%	25.00%	88%
Never					
Conducting meeting of					
women at the time of	28.57%	3.17%	69.76%	56.25%	-
planning	-	31.74%	11.62%	-	-
Many time	-	36.50%	-	-	-
Thrice at the time of	-	15.87%	11.62%	18.75%	58.33%
planning	71.57%	12.69%	6.97%	25.00%	41.66%
Thrice at the time of					
programme					
Once					
Never					

(Contd.)

(Contd. Table 11)

Activities	*Women in response about activities (%)*				
	Sukhomajri	*Rel Majra*	*Chandrabadni danda*	*Chandrabhaga*	*Fakot*
Training of women for W.S.M.	-	-	55.81%	40%	-
One training programme	-	-	37.20%	60	-
Two training programme	100%	100%	6.97%	-	100%
No training programme					
Film show for women					
One show	5%	10%	30%	15%	20%
Two show	10%	7%	70%	75%	15%
No show	85%	83%	-	10%	65%
Pre-survey of WSM and women consent	74.28%	73.0 %	83.72%	98%	62.5%
They have some idea	11.42%	9.52%	9.30%	2%	25%
No idea of survey	14.28%	17.46	6.97%	-	12.5%
Do not know about survey					
Other	-	-	-	-	-

Women's role in live stock management:

Despite the significant role played by women in livestock management and production (The 1985 Dairy India Year book estimated women's employment at 85 percent of the total employed in dairy production), women's control over livestock or its products has been negligible. Even though women handle most of the production aspects, men assume cooperative membership as they are the legal owners of the livestock. It is estimated that only 14 percent of dairy cooperative membership consists of women (MOA 1991). Income accruing from dairy activities consequently remains in the control of men who also hold the paid jobs in the co-operatives. Moreover, women invariable do not have access to training programmes in livestock management and dairying techniques which is available to men through the cooperative structure. This lowers the women's efficiency and reduces returns on investments as it is the women who handle most production aspects.

It was found that the fodder consumption was increasing and a maximum number of the families have been purchasing fodder like Turi (wheat straw) and also growing Bazara in their fields for animals. In the Relmajra and Suskhomajri, grazing system has finished and women were collecting the fodder only in the months of July and August and the distance to the forest has also reduced from 4-6 km to 1-2 km.

Women participation in WSM planning, management and monitoring is very limited. Because of social taboos, women were not attending the public meetings, but at the same time maximum women's opinion was that these meetings do not do anything because ultimately elite classes of village or powerful persons take all benefits of development projects. According to the women the following measures could increase the participation of women in development progrmmes :

(A) There should be separate meetings of men and women (Sukhomajri and Relmajra women).

(B) Formation of separate women groups at the grass root level (Sukhomajri and Relmajra women).

(C) Development agencies should appoint women motivators for motivating the farm women.

In Chandrabhaga and Chandrabadni WSM, because of women motivators the ratio of women participation in meetings was found to be high in comparison to Sukhomajri, Relmajara and Fakot WSM. In fact women participation was found to be low because of several factors like: competition for land, problems of land tenure, absence of legal entitlement of land, lack of time left after domestic and agriculture work, cultural taboos and lack of familiarity with forestry, no institutional and organizational support, women generally not invited to the meetings, not suitability of the time and location for women, women's inhibition, the lack of participatory nature of meetings, they are only for the purpose of increasing the number, women's illiteracy and lack of knowledge.

Strategies for Enhancing Women's Voices and Participation in WSM

- Participatory micro-planning (initial PRAs) with the sex ratio of 40/60 must be promoted.

- Introduction of development programmes through different tools like - demonstrations, film shows, poster exhibition and by providing examples of already developed societies, specifically for women and by the women.

- Formation of separate women groups from grass root level according to their problems and social and economic structure with special attention to weaker sections and landless women.

- Formation of local institution of women like Mahila Mandals and self help groups and HRMS.

- Training programmes for women in watershed management by the women:
  - (A) Specialized training for a group of women which will represent all the section of the society.
  - (B) This group will give training to all women of the village with the help of development agencies.
  - (C) Increasing the women staff within the development agencies like ICAR for rural women's trainings.

- The strategy of appointing a women coordinator and the successful stories from Kenya, Bangladesh, and India need to be focused while forming such strategies.

- Building alliances with other grass-root institutions like committees of Panchyats etc.

- Promoting federation of women's group.

- Local knowledge of women to be utilized in the design and selection of the place and project activities.

- Co-ordination between the different government departments like education (NLM), family planning and health etc.

- Women oriented technology pre-requisite to participatory sustainability.

- Social and technical strategies must be within the project.

- Principles of equity, women participation through HRMS and the empathy of the outside experts and timely financial help through various funding agencies.

- Attempts to be made for minimization of conflicts within the society.

- For development of the capacity for achieving participatory permanence the women staff must be technically skilled both and institutional arrangement should receive highest priority.

- Gender sensitization programmes must also be given priority.

References

Aggarwal, B. (1989) Rural Women, Poverty and Natural Resources: Sustenance, Sustainability and Struggle for change, Economic and Political Weekly, Oct 28, WS 46-WS 65.

Bansal, R.C. and Grewal, S.S., (1986), Studies on sedimentation of Sukhna lake; corrective measures and Hydrology in annual progress, report central soil and water conservation research and training institute, research center, Chandigarh.

Bourai Himanshu, Women's Participation in natural resource management, Abhijeet Publications, New Delhi, 2008.

Dhyani, B.L., J.S. Sharm, G.P. Juyal, Ram Babu and K.S. Katiyar (1997), Socio-economic analysis of participatory integrated watershed management in Garhwal Himalayas, Fakot watershed. Bul No.-35 /d-24, SWCRTI, Dehradun- 248195, Dehradun, India.

Samra, J.S. (2001) Participatory watershed management, Yojana, Vol. 45, No. 1, PP. 24-27.

Samra, Bansal, A.K. Sika, S.P. Mittal and Y. Aganihotri (1995), resources conservation through watershed management in Shiwalik Foothills, Bul. No. T-28/C-7, CSWCRTI,RC, Chandigarh-160019 (India).

Sarin, M. (1996). Joint forest Management: The Haryana Experience Centre for environment education Ahmedabad, India.

Sarin, M. (1993) From conflict to collaboration:local institutions in Joint Forest Management. JFM working paper No. 14, National support group of joint forest management, SPWD, New Delhi.

7

Measuring Women Empowerment Using Qualitative Response and Quantitative Causal Models with Conjoint-Simulation Techniques

Namrata Sharma and R.C. Sharma

Introduction

Empowering women and improving their status are essential ingredients for realizing the full potential of the social, political and economic development of the entire society. It is also necessary for achieving the goal of sustainable development. Women empowerment is not only a necessary condition for stabilizing but also to have sustainability of the development process. For realizing this objective consistent and scientific measurement of women empowerment at different levels and regions is desirable.

Women empowerment is a frequently used term in development dialogues today. A recent policy research report by the world bank (2001), identifies gender equality both as a development objective in itself, and also as a means to promote growth, reduce poverty and promote better governance. Empowerment of women is such a critical issue that has emerged as a hot topic of discussion in the various forums through out the world. For some, the empowerment of women is an active multi-dimensional process which enables women to realize their full identity and power in every spheres of life. For others, empowerment represents the ability of women to handle responsibilities, to envision a better future and to overcome the obstacles that confront them. Empowerment can be measured by using selective indicators, such as active contribution in the household, the workplace and the community. Women empowerment can also be measured through qualitative response regression model (Logit model) and quantitative multiple regression model (after measuring women empowerment index) with appropriate samples of working women. Since for overall and sustainable development of the society women empowerment is one of the essential conditions, therefore, scientific measurement of women empowerment is also desirable. Such scientific measurement with explanation of the determinants is likely to be useful for policy implications and planning in the area of women empowerment. Though a woman may be literate and working however she may not be empowered in the following aspects: domestic decision-making, financial autonomy (i.e., control over the resources), mobility/freedom of movement, child related issues, having friendship with male persons (e.g. well-being, schooling, health, marriage), and participation in the modern sector.

Review of Literature

This section deals with the review of literature of the work done in relation to different ways in which empowerment has been conceptualized and the different approaches developed to measure women's empowerment. The study by Vianelo et. al. (1990) analysed that a husband's power within marriage tended to increase in proportion to the resources that he could muster: education, income, prestige, social status, and so on. The author also found that the husband's power was associated with the stage in the life cycle and with the presence of children in the home. More importantly, wives who were employed and getting salary had more power than wives not gainfully employed. When the resource theory was applied to the study of marital power in different societies, the finding was inconsistent. Kabeer (1999) has attempted to construct the indicators of the empowerment of women, by using three-dimensional conceptual framework: (a) the 'resources' as part of the pre-dimensional of empowerment; (b) the 'agency' as an aspect of process; and lastly (c) the 'achievements' as a measure of outcomes. The study shows that the most probable indicators for empowerment of women are: family structure, marital advantage, financial autonomy, freedom of movement, and lifetime experience of employment participation in the modern sector. The study by Malhotra et. al. (2002) identifies the methodological approaches in measuring and analyzing the empowerment of women. The various indicators for measuring empowerment of women given in the study are: domestic decision-making; finance and resource allocation; social and domestic matters; child related issues; access to or control over resources; freedom of movement; and so on. Stine and Karina (2003) explain the term 'empowerment; as a process by which the dis empowered individuals and groups gain the power to control their lives and the ability to make strategic life choices. The researchers also emphasizes that the economic elements of empowerment refer mainly to the capability of earning a living. The study finds that one of the important determinants of the low average income of women is their intermittent labour force participation, which is a consequence of their time spent on unpaid work such as childcare, housework and food production. Mahendra (2004) has studied the female work participation using occupational data from the National Family Health Survey (NFHS) data set, and compared the same with the 2001 census and the National Sample Survey Organization (NSSO) data. The study finds that: (a) larger the family size the lesser is the chance for female work participation; (b) education has a positive relation with urban female work participation. The study by Kishore et al. (2004) shows the status of women's empowerment as a whole and in each of the Indian states in particular, with the help of NFHS-25 data sources. The sample of the study includes married women in the age group 15-49 from these states. The study divides the indicators of empowerment process into three sub-divisions: (a) the indicators of evidence of empowerment (through educational attainment); (b) the indicators of access to potential sources for empowerment which measures women's access to education and media exposure; and (c) the indicators of the setting for empowerment, which focuses on the circumstances of the women's lives and reflects the opportunities available to them. The study of Sridevi, (2005) analysed that the level of empowerment is higher if the educational level is similar among the women PGT teachers and their spouses. It also showed that as the level of education increases the level of conflict faced by them comes down. Also, if a woman teacher has a control over her personal salary, the decision-making power of the women PGT teacher becomes higher; it tends to have a negative effect on the level of empowerment. Rahman. M.H.,and Kazi.N, (2007) concluded that the empowerment level of rural women in Bangladesh can be significantly improved by increasing their involvement in an income generating activity such as aquaculture, providing the income goes to them and not just to their husbands. Factors such as education, extension contact and exposure to training can increase a women's technical knowledge, which in turn will increase her participation in aquaculture.

Hypotheses

The following hypotheses can be empirically tested:

- Higher the empowerment of women when staying in a nuclear family.

- Higher the age, higher the empowerment of women.
- Greater the educational qualification, higher the empowerment.
- Greater the mobility, higher the empowerment.
- Higher the support given to women by their natal home, greater the chances of empowerment.
- Higher the control over personal salary, greater the chances of empowerment.
- Higher the age difference with the spouses, lower the empowerment level.
- Higher the educational differences with their spouses, lower will be empowerment level of women.
- Higher the number of children, lower will be the empowerment.
- More time spent on household work, lesser would be the level of empowerment.
- Higher the income, higher the level of empowerment of women.

Research Methodology for measuring women's empowerment

On appropriate sampling of women the data can be collected through primary survey using questionnaire. Qualitative and quantitative information related to women empowerment and the determinants are required to be collected. The main emphasis should be on family type, age, educational qualification, household time spent, freedom of mobility, annual income of the women, spouse age difference, educational difference with spouse, number of children, control over personal salary, support from the natal home, financial decision on own health care, expenditure on education of children etc. For analyzing women empowerment qualitative response regression model i.e. Logit model and quantitative multiple regression models can be used. The determinants with their directions and magnitudes can be discussed by accepting/rejecting the various hypotheses related to women empowerment. The statistical significance of the determinants and overall relevance of the models also needs to be taken in to consideration while explaining the qualitative analysis and the multiple regressions for quantitative analysis. The variables in the models can be quantified in the forms of dummy variables, quantitative variables and scaling techniques. Dummy variables can be used for dependent variable of qualitative response model. For age, income, household time spent, spouse age difference and number of children simple quantitative information can be used. For independent variables like family type and freedom of mobility dummy variable technique can be applied. For educational qualification and educational differences with spouse, five point scaling can be used. However, for control over personal salary, supporting the natal home, maintenance of family income, financial decision on own health care, expenditure on the education of children etc. a five point scaling (0,1,2,3,4,5) shall be used, especially for constructing empowerment index based on the financial decision making power of the women. This scaling system is as follows. If the respondent is not consulted (0). If consulted (1). If, everyone decides together (2). If she consults others and decides herself (3). If she does not consult and decides herself (4). As to the methodological refinement conjoint-simulation is also very useful for qualitative and quantitative models. These iterations are helpful in optimizing the conditions of women empowerment, thereby helpful in policy implications.

Implications

The results of the empirical models, i.e. qualitative response and quantitative regression are likely to be useful in deducing some of the most crucial factors to be considered by the social planners for any policy initiatives for improving the status and empowerment of women in the selected area of research. The models are also very useful in generalizing the future research in this area. Logit model and quantitative regression are powerful and scientific methods for analyzing the women empowerment. The conjoint-simulation analysis for both the models is proposed methodological innovations in this area of research.

References

Kabeer, N. (1999), "The Conditions and Consequences of choice: Reflections on the Measurement of Women's Empowerment", *UNRISD Discussion paper* No. 108, August.

Kishor S. And Gupta K., (2004), Women's empowerment in India. In : Rajan I. and James K.S. (eds.), *Demographic Change Health Inequality and Human Development in India.* CESS, Hyderabad.

Kishore, Sunita and Gupta, Kamala (Feb. 2004), "Women's Empowerment in India and Its States: Evidence from The NFHS", *Economic & Political Weekly.*

Mahendra,. S. D. (2004), "Female Work Participation Using Occupational Data From NFHS Data Set", *Economic & Political Weekly*, February 14.

Pillai, J.K. (1995), *Women And Empowerment,* Gyan Publish House, New Delhi.

Rahman, M.H. and Kazi, N(2007), Women Empowerment through Participation in Aquaculture: Experience of a Large-Scale Technology Demonstration Project in Bangladesh, *Journal of Social Sciences* 3(4): pp.164-171.

Sridevi, T.O. (2005), Empowerment of Women: A Systematic Analysis, *India Development Foundation Discussion Paper*, June PP.1-18.

World Bank. (2001), Engendering Development: Through Gender Equality in Rights, Resources, and Voice. *World Bank Policy Research Report.* Oxford: Oxford University Press.

Vianello, Mino And Siemienska Renata, (1990), *Gender Inequality: A Comparative Study of Discrimination and Participation.* New Delhi: SAGE Publications.

8

Empowerment of Women with Reference to Women of Rural Uttarakhand

Sunita Badola

Since Independence the polity has undertaken various initiatives towards improving the socio-economic condition of women and accentuating their participation in the social, economic, cultural and educational sectors. The constitution of India enshrines the Directive Principles of state policy which have a special impact on the status and empowerment of women. The Constitution provides political equality to women through adult franchise; it was a radical departure from the traditional norms of Indian society. During the earlier period, a number of legal reforms were also made to improve the status of women through the Hindu marriage act, Hindu succession Act, Hindu Adoption and maintenance Act, Hindu Minority and Guardianship Act, Dowry Prohibition Act, Maternity Benefit Act and the like. The sixth five year plan had a chapter on women and development which sought to introduce women centered programmes for improving the socio-economic status of women. The Eighth plan furthered the move by introducing a variety of developmental programmes for women. In the national perspective plan provisions were made to increase the participation of women in the IRDP programmes to promote self employment of women. The Indira Mahila Yojna and Rashtriya Mahila Kosh gave encouragement to women to hold funds in savings, and avail them for productive activities.

Recently, the Panchayati Raj act has introduced a policy of reservation for women to not only to facilitate their participation in the political system at the grass root level but also to make them part of the decision making process in the rural parts of India. One-third of the total seats of members and heads of village Panchayats, Block Panchayats and District Panchayats are reserved for women. However, despite the many provisions women's participation in different activities, securing educational facilities and availing benefits of socio-economic development is still not very encouraging. This situation indicates towards the failure of the development programmes undertaken for improving the quality of the life of women. The socio-cultural backwardness of the traditional social system which continues to have a hold on rural India keeps the women marginalized while it opens the doors of opportunity for the males. After more than half a century since independence, the role and condition of women in rural India remains almost unchanged. Most household activities are performed by women in rural India but they suffer severe restrictions and are discriminated by employers. Such discrimination results form social values which places women in a secondary position under the subordination of men. In such system, mobility of women tends to be limited and this aggravates the discrimination against women.

What Ails Women Empowerment?

The Constitution of India enjoins upon every citizen of Indian the duty "to promote the common brotherhood of all the people of India and renounce the practices derogatory to the dignity of women". Our religious scriptures also enjoin upon us a duty to accord due respect to women and it has been said that "gods live where women are worshipped". Since long the average Indian woman has almost led a life not better than that of a slave. At all the stages of life, right from childhood to old age, she always lives in a subordinate position to man and never recognized as an independent entity free to select a course of her life or her own choice. To a wife, the only god worth worshipping is considered to be her husband, regardless of the fact whether he treats her well or bad. To look after the family and the relatives of the husband is considered her primary duty. In some social rituals the sight of woman was taken as an ominous one. The deserted women were branded as witches. Even in the modern times, in educated households also the girls are taught only duties and responsibilities, all rights belong to the boys, and hell awaits newly married woman who begets daughters and no sons. In most households women are expected to be at the back and call of their husbands, to show servility and be always at the feet of men who have every freedom to use them as shoes, or kick them away, depending upon their whims. What an irony indeed! In the same society and in the same household apartheid is practiced. There are two sets of laws: one for the privileged males and the other for the deprived tribe of women. In such an unjust society, women suffer greatly. Their physical development suffers their mental advancement and moral and spiritual growth is retarded. Their unconscious mind harbours an attitude of revolt which often expresses itself in suicides or murders. The incidence of a large number of suicides among women than men is accounted for by this factor.

The irony is that man is born of a woman, yet the latter is dominated by the former. She has been enslaved, degraded and subjected to various types of atrocities at the hands of man and the man-dominated society. Even the modern times have not brought much liberation for her. The gift of democracy which we have received from our earlier generation is denied to women, the principle of the basic equality of sexes has never been put into practice. Though, women in India were granted adult franchise long back but their counterparts in certain advanced countries have also been denied equality with the men. Even in an advanced country like the United Kingdom, adult franchise to women was given in 1928. Switzerland, which is regarded as synonymous with democracy, also accorded this right to women very late. Women in France were given the right in 1956. The record in Asian and Arab countries has been particularly dismal. The Muslims have not treated their women on a footing of equality with men. The *Shariat* does not permit women to discard Purdah. The divorce laws are heavily tilted in favour of men. Women can be bought and sold like commodities. Education has always been regarded as the sole preserve of men. All this is highly derogatory to women. To put the things in proper order vide the 42nd Constitution (Amendment) Act 1976, the Indian Parliament included in the Fundamental Duties of citizens an obligation to "renounce any practice derogatory to the dignity of women."

As the realization has dawned about the tremendous potential of women for bringing about a qualitative change in our social life, the measures for the empowerment of women are therefore being taken. Reservation for women in jobs and in all the Panchayati Raj Institutions has already been given to encourage their participation. This has produced some good results and the women taking advantage of these are showing their potential. The reservation in legislative assemblies and parliament would further improve the situation and allow the women to work for the betterment of all. Steps are being taken in government service to allow out of turn promotion to women. Girl's education is receiving top priority, with a number of Indian states already having made female education up to intermediate level free and compulsory. Measures are also being taken to make women economically self reliant in rural India. Excellence in every field of life is no longer a man's preserve. Women are asserting and trying to take benefit of the changing situation.

Education of Girls for National Development

All talk of national reconstruction is hollow without the education of women. National regeneration is possible only when educated girls remain in the forefront of national development, so far which has been a male dominated world. Women played only a second fiddle to men in all walks of life and they were condemned to the four walls of the house. However, education has given them a new confidence, the scenario is changing fast and the world is no longer the monopoly of men. More and more young women are coming forward to challenge the dominance of men. The citadel of self-claimed superiority of men is cracking. Educated girls and women are contributing to the welfare of society. Name any walk of life and you will find women excelling there. They have proved to be better doctors, scientists, artists, administrators, academicians and engineers than many of their male counterparts. However, complete literacy among women still remains a distant dream. Many conservative parents still suffer from superstitions and outdated beliefs. The percentage of women's literacy among the scheduled castes and scheduled tribes and the economically weaker sections of the society are exceptionally low. Many state governments have given some special incentives to attract more and more girls to schools and colleges. It will help in harnessing women's skills and talents for national development which actually is the need of the hour.

Reservation for Women

Women constitute almost half of humanity. It is really very unfortunate that they have to play a secondary and marginal role in the male dominated society. However, women of today cannot accept their exploitation lying down. They have launched a vigorous movement for safeguarding their rights and interests.

The bill to grant 33 percent reservation to women in the parliament has been placed in Rajya Sabha by the Congress led government of the centre, if passed in both the houses it would change the face of the parliament. As presently the parliament and the state legislatures do not have even 10 percent representation of women in them. They do not represent the aspirations, hopes and ambitious of women. Some conservative sections of our society decry the very concept of reservation for women. They consider it discriminating and violating the concept of equality which is a misconception. The constitution has provisions to safeguard the interest of the scheduled castes and other weaker sections of society, therefore the reservation for women will in no way defy the spirit of the constitution. On the other hand, it will end the marginalization of women in politics, and they would not just be conferred as a vote bank of the political parties.

A Picture of Women in Rural Uttarakhand

A study by Pande (1996) reveals that the women's input per day in the outdoor, indoor and recreational activities is generally 62.17 percent, 21.11 percent and 8.7 percent respectively in the rural areas of Uttarakhand. Women actually spend 10.25 hours a day on outdoor chores, out of a total 16.49 hours of activity. Tending to agriculture and livestock constitutes 29.35 percent of a woman's time. The study also highlights that women's drudgery is immense because of the toil associated with the collection of fuel and fodder, for which the women trudge over a long distances to carry back the load. This activity takes up 5.41 hours a day which is about 32.8 percent of the total time available. Apart from the above chores, women have to participate in social and religious functions in the absence of the male members of the family. Lacking an independent economic status and for want of control over income resources, women here are marginalized, both inside and outside the family in their socio-economic status. However, educated women are found to be better-off than those who are semi-literate or illiterate. The same study exposes the slow progress of the schemes and developmental programmes launched by government. Only a few programmes run by NGO's like Mahila Mangal Dal, Anganbari and Balwadi are women-centered, and account for improving the status of rural women. Surprisingly, the Mahila Smridhi Yojna meant for women only is also unheard of in the region. The capacity of women of the region for social change through activism, however, is astonishing. The Chipko Movement, Dharnas against liquor and the Uttarakhand movement were mainly women-led and have shown the determination of the women of the rural areas of Uttarakhand. Unfortunately these episodes come and go and their impact short lived with the result the condition and status of women remains unchanged. Out migration of men for work outside their villages or states places a heavier burden on the womenfolk who toil harder because of the absence of men. But their ability to cope up comes to the forefront at the cost of increased suffering. The overall participation of women in local and regional agitations for socially useful causes is appreciable but their achievements in the movements and agitations have also failed to improve their status and conditions.

The introduction of Panchayati Raj has brought women to seats of power as village heads and at the block level, but on account of the want of training and experience in such matters, their position remains weak and their work is undertaken by their husbands who act as the Pradnans-Pati. In such conditions the political scene is once again is dominated by men. The women Pradnans usually come from families where males were Pradhans earlier and the seat falls in the reserve category for women. Owing to such family ascendancy, the family is able to stake a claim to the seat and usually secures the same. A sample study of women Pradnans has shown that they did not find much change and improvement in their status at the home level despite being a Pradnan. However, it was found that all Pradnans whether male or female are respected at social, political and religious functions by both males and females of the community. In view of the above picture the following points emerge about the situation of women empowerment:

- Education is directly related to the empowerment of women.
- Political position empowers women but their position may be *de jure* not *de facto*.
- Despite holding office or jobs, women's domestic duties remain unchanged.

References

Chand R. and Joshi, K.C. (1992), *Constraints on Production in Himalayan Agriculture,* In: Raina, J.C. (ed.) *Himalayan Environment, Man and Economic Activies,* Pointer Publications, Jaipur.

Dhar, T.N. and Gupta, S.P. (1992). *The Himalayan States of India.* Development Profile, SHERPA, Lucknow.

Government of India, *Draft Fourth, Fifth, Sixth, Seventh, Eighth and Ninth Five Years Plans, Planning Commission*, New Delhi.

Government of U.P., *Ninth Five Year Plan (1999-2002), Uttarakhand Sub-plan, Uttarakhand Development Department, Lucknow, U.P.*

Joshi, B.K. (1984), *Energy Use in Rural Areas of Uttarakhand* in U.P., Girl Institute of Development Studies, Lucknow.

Mehta, G.S. (1995), *Constraints in the Department of Uttarakhand, Giii Institute of Development Studies, Lucknow.*

Mehta, G.S. (1996), Uttarakhand: *Prospects of Development*, Indus Publishing Co., New Delhi.

Narula, D.D. (1983), *Strategy for development of Hill Region and Investment in Infrastructure*, In: Papola, T.S. and Joshi, B.K. (eds.) *Development of Hill areas: Issues and Approaches*, Himalaya Publishing House, Bombay.

Tiwari, R.T. and Sinha, R.C. (1988), *Rural Development in India*, APH, New Delhi.

Pande P.N.(1996) Drudgery of the Hill Women. Indus publication, New Delhi, p.170.

9

Supporting Factors for Women's Participation and Success in Politics in Uttarakhand

Annpurna Nautiyal and Rakesh Negi

Women in Uttarakhand lead a highly adverse life style under most pressing, challenging and unfavorable geographical, social and economic conditions. Though they have been oppressed, under estimated and marginalized in the male dominated society however, during the last few decades, their personal, social, economic and cultural life has witnessed some transformation with improvement in women's educational standard both in rural and urban areas. As a result of this an interest among the women to participate in political, social, cultural and other activities could be witnessed. The reservation for women in the Panchayati Raj Institutions has not only allowed their entry in to politics in a large number but also generated an interest towards the political activities. Their political participation and direct association with politics have opened new vistas for them. This rejuvenation and path breaking change in the mindset of women- both in rural and urban areas of Uttarakhand, its general impact and the factors helpful in women's entry in to politics have been studied, interpreted and analyzed in the present paper.

Women's Participation in Politics

In this age of advancement in every field, women have also been witnessing a sea change in their political standing. With the result their area of work is no longer confined within the four walls of their homes but they have emerged as an important part of the political process. Due to their capabilities and multi-dimensional abilities, they have been playing a significant and productive role not only in social and economic sectors but also in the national and international forums and getting familiarized with the intricacies of the political sphere. Women's activism in these fields is a natural result of their education, improved atmosphere and awareness about self and the surroundings. Actually the sound results of political participation and political activism cannot be accomplished in the absence of awareness among the women. However it is also being observed that the level of such awareness among the women of the urban areas is greater than the women of rural areas due to the impact of education, modernization as well as the easy availability of resources. As a result of this the women in urban areas are playing a note worthy role in politics vis-à-vis the rural women. Opportunities for personal development, easy and accessible transportation and communication, educational and medical facilities have played a significant role in the socio-political awakening of the women in the urban areas. However, such change cannot be noticed universally and equally on every woman as a large number of women do not show much interest in politics. Hence, a large number of women in urban areas also remain politically as laggard as the rural women. The women who are found to be politically active are generally either associated with the ruling class or belong to a family with political background. Such women enter in active politics only by virtue of their family's support or influence. In fact in a male- dominated society like ours, women's participation in politics is still not always welcomed as the male members feel that politics is full of dangers, manipulations, complexities, insecurities and not suitable for the women as the women naturally lack in such manipulative skills therefore it becomes difficult for them to handle successfully the complexities of politics. Thus women are discouraged to participate in politics on account of the security perspective, but on the other hand men have also opposed women's participation in politics to maintain their dominance and monopoly. However under the pressure of changing socio-economic circumstances as well as on account of their capacities women have carved a niche for them in every sector and thus become equivalent of men. In view of this it is being opined that in the national political field also it would be difficult to overlook the women for a long period.

To ascertain women's presence and representation in the political arena the 73rd and 74th constitutional Amendments have played a noticeable role. By virtue of these amendments and the benefits of 33 percent reservation, in many instances the women have registered their presence effectively by their working and efficiency in the Panchayati Raj Institutions. Unfortunately despite their capacities and determination the women's negligible representation in legislative assemblies and the Parliament in proportion of their total population is a cause to worry. Serious efforts and initiatives are required to change this grim scenario. Since women's participation in politics is not easy and smooth, therefore following questions need to be analyzed and critically examined: How can women's participation and activism particularly the grass root women's participation in politics can be increased? How can other (marginalized) women become a part of such activism? Which kind of caliber and qualities are necessary for the women to be active in politics? Which factors could be supportive for women's entry in to politics? What are the conditions which make a woman's entry in to politics smooth and easy? These questions are not only important to understand the trends of participation and activism of the women of the Garhwal Himamayas in Uttarakhand but also to understand the constraints and challenges. In view of this a field survey of two districts of Garhwal Himalayas namely Rudraprayag and Chamoli districts was conducted. A sample of 450 women was randomly selected from the six villages (25 women consisting of all sections of the society and above 18 years from each village and urban area) and three adjoining urban areas from the three blocks of Rudra prayag district i.e. Augustmuni, Ukhimath and Jakholi and three blocks of Chamoli district i.e. Gairsain, Tharali and Joshi Math. In Augustmuni Block the rural villages namely Gabani, Kandara, in Ukimath block Mukku Math, Lawara gaon and in Jakholi block Sumari, Bagwar gaon and the three urban areas namely Rudra Prayag, Ukhimath, Market and Jakholi Market were selected. In Gairsain block Bhalsaion Gaon, Sainji Gaon, in Tharali block Kera, Meltha villages and in Joshi Math block Paini Gaon and Raini gaon villages and the three urban areas Gairsain Market, Tharali Market amd Joshimath Market were selected. The data in the context of the above questions was collected through the structured questionnaire and the findings of this survey are being presented in the following text.

Education, Activism and Women Empowerment

As education polishes and refines a person's personality and develops rationality, sagacity, awareness, creative thinking and evaluation, therefore, education is essential for overall development of a person. An educated person remains attentive not only to his immediate environment but also keeps sufficient information and knowledge about his rights and duties and it also affects individual's activism. This is more pertinent in the context of women and their empowerment is a far cry without education because it is only education which infuses sense of self-awareness and confidence in women, paves way for efficiency and economic independence and also enables them to participate in decision making process. In fact only through education comprehensive social and political transformation in any society can be brought and a sense of responsibility and awareness could be nourished through elementary education. (Dhasmana 1997). Due to the lack of elementary education women not only generally remain behind in the process of political development but also unaware of their rights. Though it has been noticed that in rural areas women have a natural understanding of their atmosphere and experience but the lack of education hampers the development of their personality and prohibits them to play an active role in the developmental programmes. The condition of women's education in rural areas is still deplorable and this is despite the fact that article 14 of the Indian Constitution clearly states that all girls and boys within the age group of 6-14 year will be given free and obligatory education without any discrimination. The National Education policy of 1986 had also emphasized that all children of 6-14 year age group will be given necessary education without gender discrimination but this goal has not been fully achieved. It can be ascertained from the following table.

Table - 1 Women's Literacy since 1951 to 2001 in India

Year	*Percentage*
1951	7.9
1961	12.9
1971	18.7
1981	24.82
1991	32.41
2001	54.61

Source: Census of India.

The above table clearly shows that women's literacy rate was 7.9 percent in 1951 and in 2001 it has become 54.61 percent.

Though it has increased but still the goal of 100 percent literacy (barring Kerala) has not been achieved. Even today, most women living in rural and remotest areas are illiterate. Though girls' education in rural Uttarakhand has got a momentum and overall literacy rate of women in Uttarakhand is better than the country as a whole but still women are backward in this field. Since education is the basis of an individual's overall development and awareness, therefore the educated women stand a better chance of succeeding in politics than the uneducated because illiterate women, even if elected for some political post, mostly depend upon their husbands or other male members of the family for implementation of their duties. Such women though enter in politics on account of their family's dominance but due to their ignorance and low-self-confidence they simply act as a rubberstamp. In view of this it can be said that education not only makes women's entry in to politics easy, but also their functioning effective. This is possible because educated women keep knowledge about their rights, duties and environment and can perform their duties efficiently. In the findings of this survey it was noticed that educated women could get a smooth entry in politics vis-à-vis illiterate women. Furthermore it was also observed that education enhances women's interest and

Table- 2: Impact of Education on Women's Participation in Politics

S.N.	*Respondent's View*	*Rural Women*			*Urban Women*			
		Total	*Yes*	*No*	*Total*	*Yes*	*No*	*Gross Total*
1.	Education creates interest in politics	300	94%	6%	150	96%	4%	450
2.	Educated women can easily enter in politics	300	62%	38%	150	63%	37%	450

enthusiasm in political debates, meetings and other activities as the following table shows.

The figures shown in Table 2 reveal that 94 percent women in rural regions and 96 percent women of urban background viewed that women's political activism is enhanced due to their education. They admitted that there is a direct link between enriched educational level and enhanced political activism. Besides, they also realize that educated women are efficient enough to secure political foothold for themselves. On the other hand, there are merely 6 percent women in rural areas and 4 percent of urban background who did not see any link between women's education and their level of political awareness. 62 percent women of rural area and 63 percent women of urban background opined that educated women get entry in to politics easily whereas 38 percent rural and 37 percent urban women held the view that even for educated and advanced women the entry in to politics was not easy. To their mind, women's entry in politics has always been complex because their political association is not welcomed by male dominated society. However most women respondents shared the view that educated women are respected and accepted due to their self-confidence and on account of their awareness they are able to develop strategies to confront the challenges and problems.

Relationship between Women's Personal Traits, and Their Political Participation

During the last two decades, government has initiated many programmes for women's social, economic, educational and political participation as well as their overall development. As a result of these initiatives, traditional, social and familial shackles for women in most rural and urban areas are being weakened. Today, women are playing key roles in every walk of life on account of education, self confidence and self dependence and they are also associating themselves in the mainstream of political development. It is said that progress of a particular society should be evaluated on the condition of women in that society, thinking from this perspective, women's development is significant for the progress of a society but all women can not actively participate or enter in politics nor do all have the requisite qualities to succeed. Therefore, generally, the only women who have some specific personal qualities or traits are found to be successful in politics. Whenever we discuss about empowered and successful women in political horizon; the name of only a few women are taken whose ability, leadership qualities and charismatic personality is universally acclaimed like Sarojini Naidu, Vijay lakshmi Pandit, Indira Gandhi, Sonia Ghandhi, Mayawati, Jayalalita, Uma Bharati etc. Their personal qualities have played a noticeable role in their social and political success. Actually in a social and political system personal traits of an individual like personality, tendency of adjusting with others, eloquence, sense of service, courage, organizational abilities, leadership qualities, straight forwardness, decision making ability, judiciousness, honesty and effectiveness etc. have great importance. Indian women since time immemorial- have witnessed a number of social, political and cultural ups and downs. Women, who rebelled and challenged the system by their intellect, sagacity, courage and efficiency have been subsequently honoured and recognized by our society. Kiran Bedi, Bachendri Pal, P.T. Usha and a host of other women have carved a remarkable place for themselves in their respective fields. Besides, many other women are also performing significant roles and working shoulder to shoulder with men- by virtue of their personal qualities.

The 73rd and 74th constitutional amendments have provided 33 percent reservation to the women in the Panchayati Raj Institutions. These amendments are meant to encourage political activism of the grass root women but it was found during the survey that women are still captivated by the chains of conservative thinking of the society and they also lack the personal traits and awareness which are important for leadership qualities. With the result in the absence of impressive personal qualities, real authority of women village heads was being enjoyed by men. But in the villages where women village heads had influential personality; all functions were being undertaken by them without any interference. As the following table shows that personal qualities and abilities play an important role in women's political association and activism.

Table- 3 Influence of Personal Qualities in Women Leadership in Uttarakhand

S.N.	*Respondent's View*	*Rural Women*			*Urban Women*			
		Total	*Yes*	*No*	*Total*	*Yes*	*No*	*Gross Total*
1.	Led meetings and conferences	300	5%	95%	150	14%	86%	450
2.	Family support helps political association and activism	300	5%	95%	150	9%	91%	450

As the figures demonstrated in table no. 3 reveal that only 5 percent women in rural areas have led meetings and the picture is not so bright in urban areas too where only 14 percent women chaired meetings or conferences or participated in such programmes. In the rural regions, 95 percent women informed that nobody from their family was associated with the political parties. In urban areas too, 91 percent women denied the association of any member of their family in politics. Political association of a family member is important from the point of view that it can generate an interest in other family members also in politics. Besides, personal qualities and capabilities of such persons may also encourage other members to lead political meets and rallies. But such interest and initiative was not noticed as in majority of families no one was associated with politics and political parties. The number of women interested in urban areas to participate in political meetings and gatherings were found to be larger than the women living in rural regions because of the spread of education, literacy and awareness. However 73 percent women in rural areas and 84 percent in urban regions told that they cast their vote according to their choice, only 27 percent women in rural areas and 16 percent women in urban areas told that they cast their vote as per the will of husband/head of the family. Some women even told that that they cast their vote after considerable self deliberation. Only 2 percent women in rural areas and 14 percent in urban sector accepted that caste was an important factor for them in voting. For 9 percent women in rural sector and 11 percent in urban regions candidate's educational background was the basis of giving their vote. 7 percent women of rural background and 5 percent of urban sector told that they cast their vote on the basis of regionalism. However majority of women (63 percent women in rural areas and 66 percent in urban) areas told that they give their vote on the basis of the personality of the candidate. Only 19 percent women of rural background and 17 percent of urban background admitted that they voted on the party basis. As the above analysis shows that majority of the women cast their vote on their own which can be considered a good sign and indicator of women's ability to use their discretion and take the decision without any pressure or influence. It also shows that women's thinking is changing and they are developing the capacity of weighing the things according to the merit but still there are women who lag behind and need to be helped to overcome the weaknesses.

Women's State of Mind

Since, the women of Garhwal Himalayas in Uttarakhand on account of the tough geographical and physical conditions have some natural qualities like tolerance, toughness, sacrificing nature, ability to bear sufferings, submissiveness and adaptability etc yet their sacrificing nature and submissiveness are considered as their weakness and some times lead to their exploitation also. Women also have a natural tendency to disparage them in comparison to men and due to such state of mind they are not only underestimated by the society but also denied freedom of action, choice or selection. It is ironical that due to women's inherent natural qualities on the one hand women are given the title of Matrashakti (Mother who is powerful) by the society but on the other they are denied equal rights and freedom. The World Empowerment Report has put India at 114 place as far as gender equality and empowerment is concerned whereas the small states like Cuba and Sri Lanka are far ahead of India in this regard. India is ahead of only tiny states like Nepal and Pakistan, whose report on the standard of women empowerment has been abysmal. Though it cannot be denied that, on the one hand, persecution and crime against women are fast increasing, yet to some extent by the efforts of governmental and non-governmental organizations, a positive change in women's condition can also be noticed. Despite insurmountable hurdles and many contemporary challenges, women by virtue of their judiciousness, intellect and courage are making significant advancement in almost every walk of life. Though, the number of such progressive women is far less yet, it is also being noticed that gradually women are changing their mind set and using their personal qualities, sagacity and capabilities for their betterment and even stepping in the highly complex field like politics.

The following table also corroborates this truth that despite the positive changes majority of the women in the rural areas are still suffering from some complex which does not allow them to be active in meetings or their participation in elections or considering them capable of handling challenges or holding political posts efficiently. The mind set of considering themselves inferior, weak and incapable in comparison to the male members not only hampers their growth but also deprives them from their rights as well as the decision making capacity in the family as well as outside the family.

Table- 5: Mindset and the Political Activism of the Women in Uttarakhand

S.N.	*State of Mind*	*Rural Women*			*Urban Women*			
		Total	*Yes*	*No*	*Total*	*Yes*	*No*	*Gross Total*
1.	Contest elections in future	300	46%	54%	150	44%	56%	450
2.	Efficient, desirous to work on political posts	300	44%	56%	150	85%	42%	450

In the rural areas almost 56 percent women accepted that they were not desirous of holding the political post as they did not consider themselves efficient enough for holding such positions whereas in the urban areas 85 percent women considered themselves capable enough to hold the political posts. In comparison to the women of rural sectors, women's sate of mind in urban areas is more favorable for political participation. 52 percent women in rural areas also accepted that their hesitation in expressing their views, interacting with the people or talking to the officials was also responsible for their plight in the political field. On the contrary in the urban areas only 49 percent women admitted that their hesitation hampers their efficiency and capability. The increased level of self confidence in the women of urban areas, allows them to interact with the officials or people boldly whereas, the low level of self confidence or inferiority complex prohibits the women of the rural areas. By virtue of orthodoxy and narrow-mindedness in rural regions, women's state of mind (their mental make up in general) is so captivated that they hesitate while talking to the officials or the people and generally express their opinion through their men. There was a common fear also among them that if they did something they would become a laughing stock. It was found that in the panchayati raj institutions only 22 percent women of the rural background had been performing their duties themselves, 78 percent women of the rural areas told that they perform their duties with the help of their husbands or other male members of the family, on the other hand 40 percent women of the urban areas accepted that they perform their duties themselves in the Panchayati Raj Institutions and 60 percent women told that they perform their duties with the help of their husbands/family. Though in the urban areas also 60 percent women have been taking the help of their husbands or family however the number of women discharging their duties was much larger than the rural areas. Moreover the women in urban areas were found to be taking advice or guidance from their family members but the male members were not discharging duties on their behalf. The system of Pradhan Pati was found to be present in the rural areas only. In fact women in urban areas with their enhanced self-confidence due to education and overall atmosphere were found to be coping with the fast changing scenario efficiently. On the contrary in rural areas due to the women's dependence on their husbands/families as well as their state of mind of considering themselves inferior was not allowing them to work without pressures or independently.

Women's Interest in Politics and Activism in Uttarakhand

For ensuring an independent, active and equal political participation of women, the Indian Constitution have provided equal rights to the women however, despite noticeable progress in the field of democracy and development a very significant progress has not taken place about women's participation and role in the public life. Women's role- vis-à-vis their population is still marginalized in politics and their political activism has been too limited be it elections or representation in parliament or assemblies. It was found that in most of the rural areas, aged women were generally illiterate hence their decision was determined by male members, like father/husband/son, of their family. In the absence of education and information their political activism and awareness was also very low. Surprisingly, only 2 to 7 percent women were aware of the 73rd and 74th constitutional amendments which have given them 33 percent reservation in the local bodies. (Nautiyal Annpurna, 2003) However, it was also noticed that despite their ignorance on account of the reservation women's participation in democratic system at the grass root level has been increasing and it is being seen as a blessing in disguise for enhancing women's entry or training in to politics. In fact, equal participation of men and women in every walk of life and decision making process can alone pave the way for overall development, for women's interest in politics, their participation in power and equal rights and freedom of action.

As interest in politics does not simply mean casting a vote; rather, it also means sharing power and active participation in the decision making process at every level therefore such participation is necessary for showing interest or activism in the political process. Women's interest in politics makes them aware about their rights and duties however political interest and activism of all people can never be the same. In fact political socialization of a person, public contact, access to persons and organizations, his/her atmosphere, personal interest, personality, opinion about political issues, educational level, family conditions also plays a significant role in deciding the political activism of a person. As far as the women's interest, participation and activism in politics is concerned; it is always full of complexities and social restrictions due to which very few women take active interest in political activities. Women's political activism can be increased or decreased as per their education, age, income, vocation and prosperity etc. In 1991 a total number of 8699 candidates contested general elections for 521 seats out of this the number of contesting females was only 325. Women's winning ratio in 1999 elections was 17.2 percent far ahead of men's dismal 11.4 percent. This shows that though women are capable of producing good results but in the absence of reservation in the parliament and assemblies' women's representation is still poor and it also hampers their activism and empowerment. However reservation for the women in the local bodies has at least facilitated their entry into politics and created their interest in politics as a large number of women have become active in political arena or have been made active after getting 33 percent reservation. In the survey also 38 percent women of rural areas and 56 percent women of urban areas admitted that they were genuinely interested in political activities rest of the women exhibited no interest in the political activities. Women residing in urban areas were found to be more interested and active vis-a-vis the rural women because of their education, political knowledge and awareness through the easy availability of the newspapers and other means of information and communication. Though it was also observed that many women in rural areas also take great interest and show curiosity in politics, yet their number was very small. The women's reluctance in political activities was also related to their illiteracy. In view of this it can be suggested that if

Table- 6: Women's Interest and Activism in Politics in Uttarakhand

S.N.	*Respondent's View*	*Rural Women*			*Urban Women*			
		Total	*Yes*	*No*	*Total*	*Yes*	*No*	*Gross Total*
1.	Knowledge of 73rd, 74th constitutional amendments	300	2%	98%	150	7%	93%	450
2.	Women should participate in politics	300	92%	8%	150	97%	3%	450
3.	Should work for Harassment prevention	300	33%	67%	150	24%	76%	450

these women are also given quality education and accessibility to the means of information and communication their political interest and activism could be enhanced and enriched. Almost 95 percent women in rural and urban areas take interest in casting their vote but such interest for other activities was not seen.

As the above table shows that though only 2 percent women in rural areas and 7 percent women in urban areas were aware of the 73rd and 74th constitutional amendments, which gives women reservation in local bodies but 92 percent women in rural areas and 97 percent women in urban areas supported women's entry and participation in politics. The above analysis shows that reservation which is given to women in local institutions under Panchayati Raj System is still unknown to majority of the women in rural areas. Besides, even in cities, only educated women were found to be aware of it. Most women belonging to both rural and urban had a positive response on the issue of women's entry into politics, their activism and direct participation.

However, surprisingly no noticeable role was being played by the women against the issues of women harassment. Only 33 percent women in rural areas and 24 percent women in the urban areas admitted that they made efforts for the prevention of women's harassment. No activism was shown by 67 percent rural and 76 percent urban women in this regard. The women had a common opinion that they feel hesitant in intervening in other person's private matters however, if such issue becomes public they make an attempt to resolve it. Women of rural and urban background also informed that they never got any chance to help a women suffering from harassment or exploitation, as generally women suffering from harassment prefer to suffer in silence due to the fear of defamation. Therefore, mostly such incidences remain in darkness.

Familial Support and Women's Entry in to Politics

After studying the list of women candidates in previous elections, it can be easily traced that most of them have been associated with influential or political families. There have been very few women candidates without political or influential family background (Pande and Pande, 2001) in fact women's entry in politics and their political participation becomes smoother if persons of their family are already in politics. Though generally women of all strata need family support for their entry in to politics and political upliftment, however in the urban areas the dependence of the upper and middle class women on their men can be found to be relatively low but in the rural areas the women particularly less educated and of the weaker sections and the backward classes can be found totally depended on their men for their political participation. Women at times have been seen using political power in place of their husbands. For example, in Bihar, when Mr. Lalu Prasad was deposed due to his alleged involvement in many scams, Rabri Devi, his wife became the Chief Minister of Bihar. But, despite Rabri holding the Chief- Ministerial chair, real control of power remained in the hands of Lalu Prasad. Such women do not leave any mark of their personality on any one and also fail to inspire other women. On the contrary, one can cite the example of UP Chief Minister Mayawati although she also entered in politics with the help of Bahujan Samaj Party founder Kanshiram yet she carved a niche for herself due to her hard work, good understanding and leadership qualities. Though she belongs to the marginalized downtrodden class, but on account of her personal qualities and interest in politics, she is leading a big state like Uttar Pradesh. Encountering a number of hurdles by virtue of her stringent image and will- power Mayawati has become a political paradigm for women belonging to all sections. There are exceptions but on a larger scale the political participation and activism of country's half population is still limited to only the women of royal dynasties and aristocratic sections of society. Women's participation in local bodies, legislative assemblies and parliament is not decided by their will and self decision; they are either used to secure sympathy votes after the death of their politically associated father or husband or to keep a party intact in power. For a common woman it is still difficult to enter in politics on her own without the help of her family or other influential person as right from beginning women are taught that they are incapable of taking decision and insecure without the protection, assistance and patronage of men therefore a sense of insecurity and incapability always prevails in their mind. The feeling of insecurity and dependence gives birth to an inferiority complex which takes a permanent place in the psyche of rural women who also suffer from illiteracy and gender- discrimination. As a result, ever after growing mature, they do not take their decisions independently. In such upbringing and atmosphere how can one hope that a woman would perform responsibilities of public life like politics later on in her life? Since it is important to have qualities like courage, leadership capability, ability to take free decision, eloquence, confidence etc, to be successful in politics, therefore, even after getting reservation in local self government it was found that there is a sheer lack of interest in politics and also awareness about political happenings among the women. Women representatives were essentially working with the aid and assistance of their family. Moreover, due to social reasons also women hesitate entering in politics, practically most men and even women also not favour women's entry in politics or their political activism. As a result, whenever women contest election, they do not get desired support from voters including women voters. It is also noticed that women though working actively in political parties are considered weak candidate from the perspective of winning an election. Growing violence against women, insecurity, crimes, nepotism and corruption in politics are some of the other causes for which even the educated and upper-class women were not found to be very much interested to enter in the political arena. But it was also found that if the women get support from the family they not only feel confident but perform their duties with perfection and ease because familial support not only elevates women's self-confidence but inspires them also to keep up their journey.

Table-7: Importance of Women's Opinion in Familial Decisions and Local Institutions in Uttarakhand

S.N.	*Respondent's View*	*Rural Women*			*Urban Women*			
		Total	*Yes*	*No*	*Total*	*Yes*	*No*	*Gross Total*
1.	My decision is acceptable to family	300	79%	21%	150	80%	20%	450
2.	Local bodies took my opinion seriously	300	57%	43%	150	53%	47%	450
3.	Husband's help elevate my self confidence	300	98%	2%	150	99%	1%	450
4.	I enjoy family support	300	91%	9%	150	91%	9%	450

The above table shows that 79 percent women of rural areas and 80 percent women of urban areas admitted during interaction that their decision was acceptable to their family. 57 percent women in rural sector and 53 percent in urban sector told that they are taken seriously in local institutions. Only 43 percent women of rural background and 47 percent urban women gave the negative response. Significantly, 98 percent rural and 99 percent urban women admitted that their self confidence was increased with their husband's collaboration. 90 percent women of both the areas acknowledged that their family members support them regularly in the performance of their duties. The analysis points out that women's judgment is considered important in their family and their opinion is also taken seriously in the local bodies, institutions and offices. A helping hand from their husband enriches their self confidence and their awareness level also increases which is important for playing their roles successfully.

Twentynine percent women of the rural areas and 35 percent women of the urban areas told that they perform their political, social and familial responsibilities themselves and 64 percent women of rural areas and 63 percent women of urban background informed that they perform their duties with the aid and advises or consultation of their family members. It was found that most women do not work independently and perform their duties with the aid and advice of their family men.

It was also observed that social activities in rural areas are generally observed by the men therefore due to less involvement of women they were being provided a smaller amount of support by men however, socially and politically active women admitted during interview that they get their family's support in performing their duties. It was also noticed that association with political parties or membership of some political party paves the way for political activism of the women; therefore, association with political parties also plays the role of a supporting element for women's entry in to politics.

Impact of Excessive Workload on the Socio-Political Activism of the Women

Excessive workload of the rural women emerges as one of the major hurdles for their political activism. All important domestic and agricultural work is performed by women in the rural areas of Uttarakhand because of the male migration. Their immense co-operation has made them the backbone of local agriculture and economy. Despite diverse and unfavourable geographical conditions their invaluable role in agriculture, animal husbandry, fuel and fodder management, domestic chores; conservation of water, soil and forests along other natural resources as well as nourishment of local culture and traditional, cannot be denied. The unfavourable geographical conditions of Uttarakhand make women's daily routing equally difficult and challenging. The following Table provides an idea about the daily routine of the women of the rural areas of Uttarakhand.

Table 8 : Daily Work Schedule of the Women of the Rural Areas in Uttarakhand

Daily Schedule of the Women	*Activities / Task Undertaken*
5.00 am	Getting up and bringing potable water
5.00 to 7.00 am	Feeding, Milking and caring of domestic animals
7.00 to 8.00 am	Cooking and feeding the family
8.00 to 2.00 pm	Farming/managing fuel and fodder
2.00 to 3.00 pm	Preparing lunch
3.00 to 7.30 pm	Farming/fodder management
7.30 pm	Home coming to prepare for other duties
8.00 to 10.00 pm	To preparing Dinner and feeding family
11.00 pm	Going to bed

Source: Based on observation during field survey.

As evident from the above in rural areas, most of time of the women is spent in duties like farming, managing fuel and fodder and domestic work. With such a time consuming and tough daily routine, there is hardly any time left for rest or recreation. During the interview and interaction (which hardly lasted for 20 -25 minutes) also a kind of desperation was noticed among the women because of the work still left to be attended. Working hard ceaselessly for 13 to 19 hours out of 24 is very tough for them and more so in the absence of the basic necessities of life like health, education, potable water, electricity their life has become more difficult. Prevalence of conservative social customs and superstitions also increase women's plight in hills and they remain unaware of childhood fantasies, flavour of youth and suffer from the onset of an early old age. If the daily routine of these women could be reduced undoubtedly they would be able to spare time for other activities also and register their presence on account of their personal traits of tolerance, determination, coordination, understanding and compassion.

Obviously, excessive workload is a major setback for rural women's active participation in politics. Although the urban women also look after the domestic work, family responsibility and the children but the rural women in addition to domestic work also perform the activities like farming, managing fuel and fodder etc due to which they always face the paucity of time for other social and political activities. The urban women on account of the basic facilities available get more time for viewing television, guiding the children, religious duties, daily walk, participation in meetings etc.

Conditions/Qualities/ Traits/ of Women who Succeed in Politics

The analysis demonstrates that women who belong to families which are politically active or associated with some political parties remain successful in carving a niche for themselves in politics. It was also found that women belonging to the nuclear families could be politically more active than others due their limited responsibilities. Educated women have more chances for being active in politics because the women of the rural areas of the Garhwal Himalayas in Uttarakhand have all the qualities but in the absence of the sound educational background their confidence in expressing their opinion and awareness level about the issues was found to be low. The personality of an individual and qualities like leadership capability, eloquence, self-confidence, skillfulness, rationality etc. also helps a person to secure a foothold in politics. A woman who is full of self confidence, has capability to lead meetings, political rallies and takes keen interest in politics can also get an easy entry in politics. Women in urban areas show greater enthusiasm in politics relatively to those in rural sector. As a result, women in urban areas are fast succeeding in politics vis-à-vis women of remote and rural background. Moreover, women who enjoy full familial co-operation, also enter smoothly in politics. Besides, women, who have a political background, enjoy the company and confidence of influential or politically associated persons also get a chance to enter in to politics or they actively participate in this arena. Politics is an accessible destination for women who are shrewd, judicious and full of ability to attract political parties. If viewed from historical perspective also it becomes obvious that women with the above characteristics and personality have been able to achieve political goals, offices and hence, got chance to express their abilities.

Conclusion

On account of the above supporting factors it can be noticed that most of the women from common background are still far away from the doorstep of politics and they are not seen anywhere in the race of political power sharing. Although women's participation has increased at the grass root level after the implementation of the 33 percent reservation and in Uttarakhand women have been able to capture non reserved seats also (their presence is more than 40 percent in local bodies and the Uttarakhand government has made the reservation for the women in local bodies 50 percent) but barring a few women the majority of the women are still dependent on their husbands or male members in performing their duties due to their illiteracy, inferiority complex, lack self confidence and quality education etc. Therefore, there is an urgent need to change the scenario and create such opportunities and conditions which make women's entry in to politics easy and smooth and they are also able to leave their mark by actively working for the development of their area. Women's sincerity, integrity, judgment about the needs, priorities and commitment towards duty make them a perfect candidate for bringing changes in political scenario which is full of corruption, deceit and non accountability. In view of this it is more than essential to ensure women's entry in to politics by providing them good quality education, grooming them for discharging their duties efficiently as well reserving seats for them in parliament and assemblies also.

References

Dhasmana, Rajendra, ed (1997) Sikhraj Smarika, New Delhi. p. 103.

Nautiyal Annpurna (2003) :Women and Development in the Garhwal Himalayas, *Asian Journal of Women's Studies* (Seoul) Vol. 9, No. 4.

Pande Tejeskar and Ojeskar (2001) Samaj Karya. Bharat prakshan. Lucknow. p. 570.

10

Empowerment of Women: A Case Study of District Uttarkashi in Uttarakhand

Anjali Bahuguna and M.M. Semwal

Empowerment of women is a dynamic, multidimensional process, which enables women to realize their full distinctiveness and powers in all spheres of life. Empowerment strategies consist of greater access to knowledge and resources, greater autonomy in decision making and greater ability to plan their lives, literacy and higher education, better health care for herself and her children, necessary financial and service support for self employment, opportunities for higher positions of power including governance and complete knowledge of her rights.

Education is a very important tool of empowerment and particularly women's education not only paves the way for their true empowerment but also benefits the whole of society. It has a very significant impact on poverty and development and it is also the most influential factor in improving child health, reducing infant mortality and limiting the family size too. Education enhances the women's status and decision making power within the family which is a major step towards their equality and empowerment. Low level of literacy among women leads to unequal treatment and wages in the labour market. On the other hand it is assumed that literacy of women could lead to more and better economic opportunities and better income levels which would ultimately lead to empowerment of women. According to National Human Development Report 2001, "The process of education and attainment there of has an impact on all aspects of life. It captured capability of acquiring knowledge, communication and participation in community life. It alters individuals and even community's collective perceptions, aspirations, goals as well as the ability and the means to attain them. The level and spread of education has not only been an important precondition for sustained economic growth, both in the developed and developing countries, but it has also played a critical facilitative role in the demographic, social and political transition of these societies" (Planning Commission, 2001).

The government is committed to improve the status of women in India and for fulfilling this objective besides the constitutional guarantees; several schemes and programmes have been planned and executed from time to time. The declaration of the year 2001, as the women's empowerment year was therefore, significant as it reiterated the government's commitment to bring about equality for women in all walks of life and create large scale awareness with the active participation of women themselves. It was the 6th Five Year Plan (1980-85) that can be taken as a landmark for the betterment and empowerment of the women; it is here that the concept of women and development was introduced for the first time. According to the plan, "the low status of women in large segments of Indian society cannot be raised without opening up opportunities of independent employment and income for them".

The Report of the National Commission of self employed women and women in the informal sector (1988) recommended training courses for women for skill upgradation. UNDP's Human Development Report 1995 stated, "women must be regarded as agents and beneficiaries of change. Investing in women's capabilities and empowering them to exercise their choices is not only valuable in itself but is also the surest way to contribute to economic growth and overall development. It is imperative to quote Jean Dreze and Amartya Sen," The emancipation of women is an integral part of social progress, not just a 'women's issue" (Dreze Jean and Sen Amartya 1995).

However, after discussing women empowerment, its strategies and policy implementations, the paper discusses the socio economic backwardness of rural women in district Uttarkashi of Uttarakhand which is a sparsely populated state. It has total number of 13 districts and total area is 53,484 sq.km. The density of population in the state is 159 per sq.km. as against 324 for the country. The state has 49 tehsils, 95 community development blocks and 15761 villages. According to the census 2001, the population of Uttarakhand is 84,89,349 comprising of 4,325,924 males and 4,163,425 females, the sex ratio is 962 females per 1000 males.

For the present study, 240 rural women of district Uttarkashi were selected randomly for studying the socio economic backwardness. Geographical area of the district Uttarkashi is 8016 sq.km. According to the census 2001, the total population of Uttarkashi is 2,95,013 which consist of 1,52,016 males and 1,42,997 females. The district has 1 Municipal Board, 2 Nagar Panchayats, 3 Statuary Towns, 4 Tehsils, 682 Villages, 6 Development Blocks and 388 Gram Panchayats. Historically, the people of the district have depended on a mix of subsistence agriculture, animal husbandry, and seasonal migrant labour for their livelihoods. These traditional systems are characterized by low productivity, diverse use of available natural resources (largely for home consumption), limited markets, and some aversion for innovation. The potential to generate wealth through commerce in unique mountain resources has largely been untapped by mountain residents.

The lives of hill people are intricately linked to their natural environment. Natural resource environment is degrading in many areas. Down streams effects that include high sedimentation load, floods and landslides, are increasing in some areas. Limited accessibility and lack of infrastructure to overcome the barrier of terrain and altitude are significant constraints to generating opportunities in the hilly areas. Many a times, marketable surplus and mountain niche resources have remained grossly under utilized and undervalued. A major portion of the district is hilly and forests occupy a place of prominence in the economic environment of the district. Forests of chir, oak, conifers, sal and deodar are found in the district and besides wild flowers, many herbal plants are also available in the district. The rural people have mostly the kachacha roads. Most of the people earn their livelihood through agriculture. Due to small size of holdings the farmers are not in a position to make use of modern tools and implements. Among commercial crop potato is mostly grown and gives good yield. Women out number men and perform the main functions of working force. The rural areas are under developed and poor and on account of the male migration the greatest burden of this poverty is carried by the women.

Purpose and Methodology

The major purpose of the present study was to gather relevant data regarding the socio-economic conditions of the women. The variables under the study were categorized into four broad categories.

1. **Social Indicators:**
   - 1.1 Marital Status
   - 1.2 Size of family

1.3 Occupation

1.4 Age Range

2. Educational Indicators:

2.1 Respondent's education

2.2 Training received.

3. Economic Indicators:

3.1 Income

3.2 Nature and type of expenditure

Methodology:

The sample of the present study included 240 rural women from seven villages, namely Aungi, Sainj, Bhatwari, Pala. Maneri, Kumalti and Salang from Bhatwari Tehsil in Uttarkashi district of Uttarakhand. While discussing the issues relating to re-settlement and rehabilitation of Pala Maneri Hydro electric project, the socio-economic backwardness of the women of these rural areas has also been analysed. In the present study the results are shown through frequency percentage and being presented in the following tables.

Table 1: Marital Status: Frequency and Percentage

Marital Status	*Frequency*	*Percentage*
Unmarried	73	30.42
Married	160	66.66
Widow	7	2.92
Total		.00

As the above results reveal that more than 50 percent women were married (66.66 percent) while 30.42 percent women were unmarried and a very low percentage of women constitute the third category i.e. Widow. The percentage of widow women was only 2.92 percent in these villages.

The majority of the women have a range of 1 to 9 members in their family. The percentage of this family size was very high i.e, 92.5 percent while a very low percentage reported a family size of ten or more than 10 members.

Table-2: Family Members: Frequency and Percentage

Family Members	*Frequency*	*Percentage*
1 to 9	222	92.5
10 or above	18	7.5
Total		.00

Occupation

As regards to occupation, the rural women were mainly found engaged in agricultural production and animal rearing. The main agricultural crops grown were wheat, paddy, soybean and potato and other seasonal vegetables were grown in plenty. Orange, malta, guava, banana etc. were also being produced by the villagers. Out of the 240 rural women almost 100 percent were engaged in agricultural production and animal rearing. The age range of the women sample was between 15 to 34 and above. But out of the 240 women only 3 women were in the age range of 34 and above which is very marginal (1.25 percent). While there were only 130 women between the age range of 15-24 (54.17 percent) and 107 women (44.58 percent) were in the age group of 25.34. This has been shown in the Table 3.

Table 3: Age Range : Frequency and Percentage of Age

Age Range	*Frequency*	*Percentage*
15-24	130	54.17
24-34	107	44.58
34 and above	3	1.25
Total		.00

Educational Indicators

Majority of rural women were illiterate. Therefore, the low level of education supports our standing assumption of educational backwardness among the rural women.

Table 4 : Educational Status: Frequency and Percentage

S. No.	*Educational Status*	*Frequency*	*Percentage*
1.	Up to Class V (Literate)	50	21
2.	Illiterate	190	79
3.	High School	-	-
4.	Inter	-	-
5.	B.A and above	-	-
Total			100.00

As the above table shows that only 21 percent women were literate and the rest 79 percent were found to be illiterate. The respondents did not provide any information about any skill development training or course etc. therefore no table has been prepared for the indicator training etc.

Income and Occupation

All respondents were engaged in agricultural work besides their usual domestic work. As regards the income, the households did not have any regular income. Since male members had migrated to the plains and far off places therefore either the families had been receiving money orders or cash during the visits of the migrant members to their native places. On the basis of agricultural production and animal rearing the income has been assumed below Rs. 500 and above which has been shown accordingly in the following table.

Table 5 : Income Frequency & Percentage

S. No.	*Income*	*Frequency*	*Percentage*
1.	Below Rs. 500	180	75
2.	Above Rs. 500	60	25
	Total		.00

The Above table shows that out of 240 rural women 180 had income below Rs. 500 while only 25 percent rural women had income above Rs. 500 and above this clearly indicates the financial backwardness of the women of this area.

Nature and Types of Expenditure:

This indicator was measured through two items, i.e., joint expenditure and secondly self dependence. The following table shows that 230 (96 percent) women were spending their income jointly while 10 women (4 percent) were self dependent and earning their own income. The result of Table 6 highlights the conclusion that women earn jointly and spend jointly and only a very small percentage of women were self dependent.

Table 6 : Type of Expenditure: Frequency and Percentage

S. No.	*Expenditure*	*Frequency*	*Percentage*
1.	Joint Expenditure	230	96%
2.	Self Dependent	10	4%
	Total		100.00

It has been observed that the women have to face economic deprivation and the socio-economic condition of women of this district is quite backward. Low level of education, lack of training and skill formation, low percentage of economic self dependence, low motivation for occupational mobility and unrewarding household activities lead to socio-economic backwardness.

Conclusion:

The process of empowering women in these remote rural villages could be achieved only through a better approach for action through:

- Creating an environment, through positive economic and social policies, for the development of women to enable them to realize their full potential.

- Eliminating discrimination against women and the girl child.
- Ensuring access to health care, quality education at all levels, career and vocational guidance, employment and equal remuneration.
- Strengthening legal system aimed at the elimination of all forms of discrimination against women.
- Changing societal attitudes and mindset for eliminating discrimination against women.
- Providing equal access to participation and decision making for women in social, political and economic life of the nation.

It becomes clear from the above discussion that the Eleventh Five Year Plan will not only strengthen but will speed up the ongoing process and efforts of empowering women. At the same time the Uttarakhand Government's decision to give fifty percent reservation to women candidates in Panchayati Raj Institutions in Uttarakhand is an important step for empowerment of women.

References

Planning Commission (2001), Govt. of India, National Human Development Report 2001.Oxford University Press, P. 48.

Government of India, Planning Commission, Sixth Five Year Plan (1980-85), Chap. 27, p. 423.

Shramshakti (1988), Report of the National Commission on self employed women and women in the informal sector, p. 170.

UNDP (1995), Human Development Report 1995, Oxford University Press, Delhi, p. 2.

Dreze Jean and Sen Amartya (1995), India Economic Development and Social Opportunity.

Oxford University Press, New Delhi, p. 178.

Website: http://www.jagran.com/jre/jrc.htm.

http: www.icimod.org/news/index.

11

Impact of Education on Women Empowerment in Uttarakhand

R.N. Gairola

Women empowerment has been quite a popular and comprehensive issue since a long time. People all around the world have been speaking of this phenomenon. But generally when we talk about women empowerment a question naturally arises as why we need empowerment of women? Are they less empowered? Do the women really need power? These are some fundamental questions which confront the people of the world. The issue of the women empowerment is basically related to women's development. But in terms of every set of indices of development and socio-economic status the women have fared worse than men in all regions and in all strata of population. In work, employment, earning, education, health status and decision making powers, there is a clear difference between the male and the female entitlement. (Manas Chakrabarty and Yang Lahmn Bhutia, 2007) That's why the subject of women empowerment has become vital and crucial issue of modern civilized society. Today it is clearly understood that there can be no real democracy and no true people's participation in governance and development without the equal participation of women with men in all spheres of life and levels of decision making.

Meaning of Women empowerment

"Empowerment is a process that enables women to gain access to and control of material, intellectual and human resource. Empowerment is the re-distribution of the power that challenges patriarchal ideology and male dominance". (Syamala Devi and G. Lakshmi, 2005) According to the popular parlance it means the decision making capability at familial, social, economic and political areas of life that affects her individually, which in turn would lead to the sense of identity, recognition of women's contribution and knowledge to become economically independent and self reliant, to get the power to control resources like land and property.(Subhamitra Das, 2007)

Development is an integral process for promoting a better quality of life in economic, social, political, cultural and moral aspects. But so far as the development of women is especially concerned in last few years the emphasis has shifted from development to empowerment. Our policy makers have under scored the need for women's empowerment for country's progress. It has been now recognized well that women hold the key to sustainable development. So the rights of the women should be safeguard and efforts should be to empower them at all levels. In this way women empowerment is a multidimensional phenomenon, which include many issues like education, employment, health care and maternity, legal rights and sense of equality among men and women. According to Mahatma Gandhi, "Women is the companion of man, gifted with equal mental capabilities. She has right to participate in every minute detail of the activities of man. She has an equal right to freedom and liberty as him. She is entitled to a supreme place in her own sphere of activity as man is in his." (Narayan Reddy, Vijay Kumar and S. Nalani 2005) Women continue to face inequality in all spheres of their life. Though women constitute half of the world's population, two third of world's labour force, but they are not getting what is their due. So empowerment of women is important as its benefits will be felt not only by the women themselves, but by the society and the nation as a whole.

Role of Education in Women Empowerment

Education is one of the most important factors which have a bearing on the thought patterns and the personality structure of his/her rights, responsibility and obligations. Education of women is of paramount importance. The movements for improving women's status all over the world have emphasized the value of education as an instrument for elimination of discrimination on grounds of sex. (Bhawana Jharta, 1998) It is believed that education will bring about a reduction in the inequalities between sexes as well as improve and uplift women's subjugated position in the society. Since education helps women to take independent decisions or make choices from the alternatives available therefore, the educational status or literacy of the women in any society is closely related to their empowerment, progress and development.

Women's Literacy in Uttarakhand

Literacy is considered an important parameter of development of any society. The higher the literacy the higher is the development. Higher level of education and literacy leads to a greater awareness and also contributes in improvements of economic conditions. In this context female literacy is considered to be a more sensitive index of social development compared to overall literacy rates. According to 2001 census report the total literacy rate in Uttarakhand is 72.28 percent, male literacy is 84.01 percent, while female literacy is 62.26 percent. Literacy rate in Uttarakhand is well above the national average of 65.38 percent. The total male literacy in India is 75.85 percent and female literacy is 54.16 percent. In view of these figures it can be said that Uttarakhand is one of the better literate states of Indian and has shown continuous rise in literacy rate since 1951 (See Table no. 2). Till 2001 the literacy rate has increased three times (from 18.93 percent in 1951 it has become 72.28 percent in 2001). But when we compare the male and female literacy rate, the situation of total female literacy can not be said to be satisfactory as female literacy has remained very low since 1951 which can be ascertained from the following table. We are still far off from the goal of 100 percent literacy rate for the females.

Table 1: Literacy rate and Gender gap in India (1951-2001)

Year	*Persons*	*Male*	*Female*	*Gender Gap in Literacy*
1951	18.33	27.16	8.86	18.30
1961	28.30	40.40	15.35	25.05
1971	34.45	45.96	21.97	23.99
1981	43.57	56.38	27.76	26.62
1991	52.21	64.13	39.29	24.84
2001	65.38	75.85	54.16	21.69

Source: Census of India, 2001.

The data presented in the above table reveals that while the literacy rate of both male and female have improved since independence, but the gender gap in literacy still persists. Since 1951 to 2001 the gender gap in literacy has remained more than 20 percent. Though as shown in the above table that in 2001 the female literacy rate has become 54.16 percent while male literacy rate has become 75.85 percent, which is about 20 percent less than that of the male literacy.

The Table 2 elaborates the male female literacy rate and the gender gap in literacy in Uttarakhand. The table shows that the literacy of both male and female as against the all India figures have improved since 1951. This improvement is

Table 2: Literacy Rate in Uttarakhand (1951-2001)

Year	*Total literacy Rate*	*Male literacy Rate*	*Female literacy rate*	*Gender gap in literacy*
1951	18.93	32.15	4.78	27.37
1961	18.05	28.17	7.33	20.84
1971	33.26	46.95	18.61	28.34
1981	46.06	62.35	25.00	37.35
1991	57.75	72.99	41.63	31.16
2001	72.28	84.01	60.26	23.75

Source: *Census of India, 2001.*

more significant in case of female literacy which increased from 4.78 percent in 1951 to 60.26 percent in 2001 as of 8.86 percent and 54.16 percent of all India figures respectively. However, in Uttarakhand also the gender gap in the literacy rate still persists although it has reduced from 27.37 percent in 1951 to 23.75 percent in 2001.

Table 3: District wise Literacy Rate (2001)

S.No.	*District*	*Male Literacy*	*Female literacy*	*Total*
1.	Uttarkashi	84.52	47.48	66.58
2.	Chamoli	89.89	63.00	76.23
3.	Rudraprayag	90.73	59.98	74.23
4.	Tehri Garhwal	85.62	49.76	67.04
5.	Dehradun	85.87	76.22	78.96
6.	Pauri Garhwal	91.47	66.14	77.99
7.	Pithoragarh	90.57	63.14	76.48
8.	Champawat	88.13	54.75	71.11
9.	Almora	98.15	61.43	74.53
10.	Bageshwar	88.56	57.45	71.94
11.	Nainital	87.39	70.98	79.60
12.	U. Singh Nagar	76.20	54.16	65.63
13.	Hardwar	75.06	52.60	64.60
Total Uttarakhand			60.26	72.26

Source: *Census of India, 2001.*

Table 3 shows that out of 13 districts, five districts namely Chamoli, Dehradun, Pauri, Pithoragarh and Nainital have recorded more than 75 percent of population as literate. Rudra Prayag, Champawat and Bageshwar have more than 70 percent population literate. But Uttarkashi, Udham Singh Nagar and Haridwar have 65 percentage of their population in this category. Female literacy rate is highest in Dehradun (76.22 percent) and lowest in Uttarkashi (47.48 percent). Three districts of Uttarakhand state i.e, Dehradun, Nainital and Pauri Garhwal have recorded more than 65 percent of females as literate. While Uttarkashi, Tehri, Champawat, Udham Singh Nagar and Haridwar district have recorded half of their female population as illiterate. Table 3 indicates worrisome picture of literacy in Uttarakhand- the large gender gap of 23.75 percentage point. Though female literacy has taken a large leap since 1951 when it was only 4.78 percent but still a wide gulf can be noticed in male-female literacy rates. As far as gender gap in literacy is concerned it is 37.5 percent in case of Uttarkashi and 14 percent in case of Dehradun district.

Table 4 indicates the rural-urban disparity in case of literacy. It is evident from the figures shown in this table that on the whole urban population has 12.56 percent higher literacy rate as compared to rural population but in case of females this difference is more pronounced. The 2001 census data shows that the gender gap of rural population is more than 27 percent while it is only 12.43 percent in case of urban population. So far as the gender gap in literacy in the rural areas of the different districts of Uttarakhand is concerned according to the 2001 census report the higher gap is in Dehradun (18.85 percent). Besides Uttarkashi, Tehri (37.50 percent), Champawat (39.38 percent), Rudraprayag (31.05 percent), Bageshwar (31.7 percent), and Almora (30.16 percent) are other districts where gender gap in literacy is very high. While in the rural areas of Dehradun, Nainital and Udham Singh Nagar, the gender gap is comparatively very low.

Table 4: Rural and Urban Gender Gap in Uttarakhand (2001)

Districts	*Gender gap in overall Literacy*	*Gender gap in Rural Areas*	*Gender gap in Urban Areas*	*Gap with in female literacy rate by residence (Urban and Rural)*
Uttarkashi	37.04	38.45	15.45	33.38
Chamoli	26.89	28.55	11.99	21.45
Rudraprayag	31.15	31.05	1.63	20.67
Tehri Garhwal	35.86	37.50	10.86	32.58
Dehradun	14.65	18.85	10.77	18.03
Pauri Garhwal	25.33	27.24	9.72	18.93
Pithoragarh	27.43	29.42	11.00	23.94
Champawat	33.38	36.38	11.52	20.75
Almora	28.72	30.16	6.79	29.37
Bageshwar	31.11	31.7	8.81	25.20
Nainital	16.41	20.03	9.84	9.55
U.Singh Nagar	22.04	24.42	16.97	12.38
Hardwar	22.45	26.41	13.63	26.36
Uttarakhand	23.75	27.22	12.43	19.25

Source: Census of India, 2001.

The data in table no. 4 shows the gender gap in literacy in the urban areas of Uttarakhand also. In this regard it is evident from the data presented in this table that in the urban areas of district Udham Singh Nagar (16.97 percent) Uttarkashi (15.45 percent) have very high gender gap, while district Rudraprayag has the lowest gender gap of 1.63 percent. Table No 3 and Table 4 also indicates that the districts with high literacy rates such as Dehradun and Nainital also have high female literacy and low gender gap. The issue of gender gap in education is most challenging and needs to be reduced. because, such type of disparity is an obstacle for women empowerment and regional development of Uttarakhand.

Conclusion

As the empowerment of women means gaining control and power over their own lives, awareness raising, building self confidence, expansion of choices, increased access to education, information, communication, control over resources and capacity building. In view of this there is need for a realignment of power at every level, more involvement in decision making at the household level, institutional and all other levels of society for promoting real empowerment of the women. Hence, women's empowerment is closely associated with women's development. Education is positively related to women empowerment and development. Better educated women generally possess good knowledge of their rights and duties; they take more part in political activities as they also possess higher political knowledge and awareness. In fact highly educated women feel politically more efficacious as compared to the less educated and uneducated. They do not find being a woman a serious handicap in solving their problems or in taking an active part in different social and political activities. Normally, highly educated women do not hesitate approaching the concerned authorities directly for solution to their problems, while less educated or illiterate women lack such quality. In this way the gender disparity in literacy seems great hurdle to women empowerment.

So far as gender disparity in literacy in Uttarakhand is concerned, lack of proper schooling facilities for the girls, lack of importance to female literacy, domestic and agricultural workload of the females could be taken as the main causes of the gender gap in literacy. In view of this it is necessary to pay special attention to female education so that the gender gap in female literacy could be reduced. No doubt spread of education among girls will help inculcate values, attitudes and orientations leading to socialization of women especially women of rural areas. Thus, instead of formal and token empowerment, it will led to real empowerment. But to achieve such goal women education must be meaningful and relevant. It must reflect the overall needs of the society and fulfill the diverse need of the society. In this way education can become potent instrument of women empowerment in Uttarakhand.

References

Manas Chakrabarty and Yang Lahmn Bhutia, (2007) Empowering Indian Women in the new wake of Globalization, The Indian Journal of Political Science, Vol. LXVIII, No. 1, Jan-March, p.115.

D. Syamala Devi and G. Lakshmi, (2005) Political Empowerment of women in Indian legistature; A Study, The Indian Journal of Political Science, Vol. LXVI, No. 1, Jan-March, pp. 75-76.

Subhamitra Das, (2007) Women and Empowerment; Predicament or Affirmative Action, The Indian Journal of Political Science, Vol. LXVIII, No. 1, Jan-March, p. 123.

Narayan Reddy, Vijay Kumar and S. Nalani, (2005) Women and Development: Challenges and Achievements, (Serial Publications- Delhi) p.1.

Bhawan Jharta, (1998) Women and Politics in India, Deep and Deep Publications, New Delhi, p. 153.

12

A Reflection on the Moral Strategies to Address the Gender Bias

Indoo Pandey Khanduri

The gender bias that prevails in the society in its approach, attitude and strategies towards the women component is the greatest obstruction in the way of women's empowerment. The attempts for women empowerment and eradication of the gender bias are closely related as both require a radical change in the distorted attitude of the society that could help reduce the gender bias and free the women from the category of second sex in the existing social structure. Further, the attitude change requires moral strategies and commitment at the grass root level. The present paper aims at exploring, analyzing and suggesting the moral strategies for reducing the gender bias approach, attitude and thinking which could pave the way towards the positive attempts for women empowerment. However, before we reflect upon the moral strategies, we need to understand the meaning of gender bias and its roots. It is also essential to analyze the results of the gender bias and its adverse impact on the attempts of women empowerment. It is with above ends in view, the present paper has been divided into three parts. The first part of this paper will try to look at the meaning of gender bias, root causes and also to trace its origin in the very social structure. In the second part of this paper, an attempt would be made to explain how gender bias could harm not only the cause of women empowerment in terms of planning family, upbringing of children and opportunities to groom their own personality and potential but also the national development as a whole. It becomes instrumental in devaluating the worth of women folk by restricting them to perform religious rituals on several occasions. In the third and concluding part of this paper, the impact of the strategies of RAP group theory, egalitarian and liberation ethics in addressing the gender bias and women empowerment and also the work to be done at ground for empowerment of the women would be undertaken and examined.

PART ONE

It is generally reflected that the problems related to the women's survival, existence, respect, growth and status are rooted in their economic status and power but a deep analysis of the issue reveals that the above problems apart from the economic conditions, are also caused by the existing social structure, religious and dogmatic practices. One can say that the thinking of gender bias is the result of persisting socio-economic conditions, but the objective analysis of the issue shows that the gender bias is already a fundamental and existing reality which is deepening and furthering the gender disparity. Thus it appears to be a vicious circle which needs to be addressed properly not from the single approach and direction. The breaking of the nexus of the vicious circle of gender bias requires attempts which have to be made at both the levels: rectifying philosophical theorization which has been used for exploiting women folk in the society and reducing the on going exploitation and subjugation of the women. This is so because if the theories are formulated with biased approach for particular objective, it will yield the biased results in practice.

But before analyzing the vicious circle of gender bias and existing realities of suppressing women-folk and examining the root causes of gender bias thinking, it is necessary to understand the meaning of bias in general and implications of gender bias attitude with particular reference to the women's problems. The Dictionary explains 'Bias is the lenient view towards a person or entity belonging to a particular section like gender, color, locality, believes or any such specialty which may lead to take a decision against the truth, to favor such person. A bias can be for or against a section.' In addition, it states that 'Gender bias is the prejudice in action or treatment against a person on the basis of their sex, for example the payment of lesser salary to weaker sex workers. What was once thought of as gender-bias has moved into an updated term of gender inequity' (definitions/gender-bias.htm). The definition of bias attitude indicates that there must be at least two groups—stronger and weaker. The historical evidences amply show that the perceptions and strategies have been developed to benefit the stronger group by exploiting the potentials of weaker group. Being more specific the definition of gender bias thinking clarifies that the stronger group of male have the feeling of superiority and for marinating their primary position they devoid the women of their due rights merely on the basis of sex and also consider them weak. The decision of determining the components of strong and weak is also not based on the ground realities but it is merely fabricated and manipulated through the pro male strategies of the male dominated societies. The very basis of considering women as weak segment of the society may exhibits the real picture in the following way. The women have been considered weak or second sex in the society on the following three bases. Firstly, women are taken to be physically weak. Secondly, they are believed to be emotional and not rational and, thirdly they are also considered incapable of taking the objective decisions. But these foundations for determining the women as the second sex have been thoroughly proven wrong by the commendable works and achievements of the women which clearly show that there is no logic or reality behind the bases of considering the women as weaker section of the society. The three myths have been intentionally developed across the world for using and exploiting women for the benefit of the male dominated society. Let us examine all the three bases one by one.

The notion of the physical weakness of women in comparison to the male, because of their reproductive ability has been narrated in the following words; '... the biological factors connect women with child bearing which makes her weak for the time being and there upon paves the way for her exploitation. Thus the base of gender discrimination is inherent in biological structure' but, it could be countered by saying '... the biological discrimination can be conditioned and it is only temporary. Women should have the same opportunities as men to make most of the abilities they have. ' (Singh, Abha 2005). It is true that the natural facts cannot be overlooked but this should never be the basis of gender discrimination rather the child bearing period of the women needs care and protection. For the positive perspective it should be accepted that the nature through the biological structure has bestowed women the childbearing capacities and this particular strength could never be taken as her weakness. This is rather a peculiar strength attributed only to her to add new strength to the nation as well as the world and could not be a basis for considering her weak for her entire life and restricting her from opportunities.

The second basis for considering women weak is that they act on the basis of emotions and not on the basis of reasoning. But in our surroundings, we can see that women despite being emotionally vibrant in the different relationship mostly take the decision for broader welfare and not for the narrow self interest. Our ethics also advocate working towards the goal of broader welfare therefore how this particular quality of women could be taken as a sign of weakness? The sacrifice of self interest for broader welfare of the family and society is the peculiar quality of women which cannot be treated as a sign of weakness because in the historical records also the sacrificing natured people have been respected and considered great. But in the case of women being emotional and sacrificing the self- interest has been used as pseudo theoretical base for considering her as the weak part of the society. Related with the second basis, the third argument is that emotions obstruct any one from taking the objective decision. Therefore it is argued that women being emotional cannot take objective decision and are also not capable of sharing the responsibility of male counter parts in the society. But this perception is also baseless as the very nature of human being is constituted of emotional and rational factors. Besides, women are equipped with strong intuitive ability to see the long term consequences and implications. In the most critical conditions women have shown their power of taking tough decisions and arriving to their goals successfully. But most of the time the male members for asserting their superior positions in the family and maintaining the trend of male domination on the wrong grounds do not respect the women's opinion. Due to such conditions it is propagated that the women cannot take objective decision which we find is a totally baseless assumption.

After exhibiting the kinds of myths working behind the approach of gender bias in the male dominating society, it becomes necessary to analyze the sources which create and enhance these kinds of biases in the society. The population studies and researches emphasize that the roots of bias thinking lie in the economic conditions however a deeper analysis shows that sources of bias are also found in the existing social structure, religious dogmatism, theoretical assertions about the personality traits and metaphysical bifurcations. How these causes are multiplying the ways of women exploitation and subjugation is a matter of serious probing? Since in the male dominated and patriarchal society women are denied any power either economic or social, thus they do not have many opportunities and means for bringing any change in their situation. Due to the lack of direct access to resources, they have the least opportunities to emancipate themselves in terms of physical growth, mental strength or emotional stability. In fact in the male dominated societies, opportunities for education, exposure and means of production were preferably provided to the male members only. The social system in the male dominating society thus ensures that opportunity is denied to female sex and this makes the women weak. It is a vicious circle of making a particular sex weak by denying opportunity to her and propagating her weakness. More so the economic factors, social traditions and religious dogmatism further contribute for the exploitation of the women. Superior social status of the male and certain ritual performance in the worshiping trends also increases the possibility of women's subordination to male counterparts. Thus it is not only economic conditions rather social and dogmatic religious practices also which assures women's weak position in the society and superiority of the men.

In the male dominating society certain theoretical assertions have also strengthened the gender bias attitude against the women. Theoretical assertions of gender biases are based mainly on the three factors of thinking; value hierarchal thinking, value dualism and logic of domination. The value hierarchal thinking or mindset focuses attention on up and down categories that confer value, status and prestige more on the up category than the down one. For example, the way human beings enjoy higher value and status than other species of the biotic communities just in the same manner the male counterparts also enjoy the higher value and status in comparison to their female counterparts. Thus, the way human beings are morally allowed to oppress or subjugate other species, the males are also allowed to oppress or subjugate women. Nevertheless, we must keep in the mind while applying the same thinking that there is a difference between the two. The argument of superiority conferred on the human beings is based on the rationality but in the case of male and female both have the rationality therefore the same yardstick cannot be applied.

The second distinctive feature of the oppressive conceptual framework is value dualism (Das, Arpana Dhar 2005) that admits disjunctive pairs in which the disjunctions are seen as oppositional rather than complimentary, exclusive rather than inclusive. Accordingly, one disjunction enjoys superiority over the other. To make it clearer, if the human beings are classified into male and female, the disjunctive value-dualism bestows higher value and status to male who are considered similar to mind and reason than to female who are identified as bodies and emotions. But this classification of men and women is not justified because the above interpretations have followed the wrong path to serve their hidden objective of male dominating society. Nowhere women are equated with bodies or physical elements of the individual and men as mental capacities. Rather both are human beings and their existence itself presupposes the amalgamation of mind and body, sensation and reason. This again cannot be the theoretical basis for advocating women's subordination in the society. The third theoretical feature of exploitative trend is the logic of domination that justifies subordination or domination of one species by the others. However the logic of domination (Das, Arpana Dhar 2005), is not just a logical structure, it involves a substantive value system and the justification of domination is based on some alleged characteristics possessed by the upper group. For example, in case of human beings, the alleged characteristics of male is rationality and therefore his domination over the female, but women lacking this special alleged characteristics i.e. rationality is wrongly justified. As explained above that male cannot be considered superior for having rationality and the logic of domination on the basis of this cannot be applied here. It is again the pseudo theoretical formulation to maintain the male domination in the society.

The above three features of thinking persisting in male dominating society forms a kind of belief which encroach not only males but also females as it has been expressed 'women have been nurtured in the belief that man by nature is better informed, can counter violence, can provide a shield, safety and securities. These beliefs are well ingrained in women; they have accepted that because of the difference in sex, nature has ordained for them only the secondary subservient roles that are derived according to the expectations of men. As secondary roles do not have a direct economic value, those who perform these roles are not counted productive. Hence, the woman's value in her eyes is much less than that of a man. We can therefore understand why the life of women was never valued highly. Its worth is dependent on the convenience or contribution she could make to man in the form of helping him to realize his roles and satisfy his desires.' (Singh, Abha 2005) The above narration of belief directed by the gender bias approach reflects two very serious implications. The first implication is the acceptance of women's inferiority and thereby their secondary role. Designating the secondary role to the half of the population implies the denial of the facilities, opportunities and growth to them. If the sufferer accepts the sufferings as the reality which cannot be changed then any effort to combat the gender bias approach and attempt for women empowerment would only be imagination and dreams. In addition, if this remains a reality, the havoc created by the bias cannot be mitigated. The women subordination, exploitation and subjugation rooted in the gender bias thinking of the male dominating society has resulted in the visible consequences, which is discussed in the next part of this paper.

PART TWO

The gender bias thinking of male dominating society has adversely affected the interest of women folk in terms of their existence, survival and growth. Apart from this it has been providing lofty foundations for wrong theoretical formulations for the exploitations and subjugation of women. The declining sex ratio, increasing deaths of girls and female feoticides are the crude results of gender bias attitude. The population studies and researches have focused their attention mainly on declining sex-ratio and unequal distribution of resources. But the adverse implications of gender bias attitude is not limited to the decline of sex-ratio and unequal distribution of resources rather it damages the objective of the overall national development. On the cultural and religious fronts it provides a secondary status to demoralize women in day to day routine. The economic implication of adversely affecting the national development is also quite natural because if half of the population is denied equal opportunities to develop and grow in accordance to the hidden potential and become quality human resources they would not be able to contribute their share of responsibilities. The issue of declining sex ratio has been more serious issue in the present times than it had been earlier. The overall difference between the male and female may be clearly shown by the recent census reports. In 1991 the sex ratio- women per thousand male was 964 but the 2001 census has shown a drastic decline to 934. The recent report of Central Medical Commission again exhibits the considerably declining rates. The report shows decline across the states and particularly all thirteen districts of Uttarakhand show the decline between 20 to 50 females per thousand male. In 2004, the PNDT (Pre- Natal Diagnostic and Test) committee was given more power in terms of taking strict action against the parents, medical persons and private practitioners who in anyway had been found to be associated with the female feoticides. However, the gross root reality indicates that the girl infants are not surviving and female feoticides is not permitting them to take birth or to take a shape of life. In other words, gender biases have killed all the humanistic approach to save half of the world.

The second visible result of the gender biases is the unequal distribution of available resources, let it be food, nutrition, education and medical facilities as well as opportunity to grow and opt for career, usually the male child gets preference over girl child. Consequently physically, mentally and social as well as family status wise they are considered to be the second class citizens and have less freedom to choose and opt their ways. Unless the gender bias is addressed, the dream of equal distribution of resources cannot become a reality and the equal level of good cannot be achieved as writes Amartya Sen; "Equal distribution of primary goods is practically not possible due to their different status in the society". (Sen, Amartya 1998) The fact should be kept in the mind that equal distribution of the resources, status and freedom are related to the achievement of common goods in the society, as it has been further said; "... making comparison of the primary goods different people have, is not quite the same as comparing the freedoms actually enjoyed by different persons, even though the two can be closely related. Primary goods are means of freedom, but they cannot represent the extent of freedom, given the diversity of human beings in converting primary goods into the freedom to pursue their respective objectives. Given the variation in sex, age, inherited-characteristics, environmental differences etc. that prevail among and within groups of people, unequal distribution of primary goods may go with the very unequal levels of freedom." (Sen, Amartya 1998) It has been rightly pointed out that freedom and equal good though are not the same yet closely related and support each-other. As mentioned earlier that the decline in the sex ratio and unequal distribution by the male dominating society harm not only the interest of women but it also affects adversely the overall national growth and development in terms of judging the per capita income as the report by the World Watch reflects "During the 1980s, per capita income dropped in at least 50 countries. A new study points to a surprising reason for the growing impoverishment of many developing nations: discrimination against women, reinforced by conventional strategies of economic development". (Jodi L. Jacobson 2007) The discrimination against women folk, especially in the subsistence economies of the Third World, is the single most important cause of population growth as well as a leading cause of poverty. Birthrates will decline voluntarily—and poverty rates drop—only when steps are taken to increase women's control over economic resources. This is so because women are the primary breadwinners in subsistence economies, which include 3 billion of the world's 5.5 billion people. Researches show that they work for longer hours and devote a larger share yet women's efforts to support their children are all too often stymied.

The Gender bias approaches in subsistence economies are ranging from wage discrimination to exclusion from developmental programmes to legal barriers to owning land to systemic violence against women. This discrimination exacerbates poverty by preventing hundreds of millions of women from obtaining credit, education, training, health services, childcare, and legal status needed to improve their prospects. As a result, not only do families remain poor, but also the economies of many Third World nations lag far below their economic potential. Men are more likely to earn cash income than women are, but they are less likely to spend their earnings on family maintenance—food, shelter, clothes, health care—and therefore less likely to pull their families out of poverty. A research in Mexico shows that women contribute 100 percent of their earnings to the family budget while men contribute at most 75 percent of theirs, and often less. It is not only the declining sex-ratio, unequal distribution of available resources and visible implications of affecting national growth adversely but the gender bias attitude also affects and disturbs the social dignity and religious freedom of the women folk. The social and religious subordination and subjugation of women can be clearly found in the rites and ritual across the country. One important example could be cited from the remote hilly areas of Garhwal himalayas where the women act as the backbone of the economy, possess immense tolerance, intellect, high level of coordination but the gender disparity does not allow them to use their full potential and also be the full part of the developmental process. The women's lack of literacy, migration of the male population, tough topography and the environmental degradation intensifies the problems of the women in the hill areas and also place them in the secondary status. Moreover when the fabric of the society is such that the women are considered subordinate to men in every respect it is obvious that women would be denied opportunities whether related to social or religious, economic or political matters. In these areas women are not allowed to be the complete part of the Nanda Devi Raj Jat Yatra, a religious procession symbolizing the journey of the mother Goddess Nanda from valley to the high mountains. It is ironical that after the procession reaches a certain height, the women are not allowed to accompany the religious journey which is undertaken to worship the Goddess Nanda, a woman herself. There is a kind of dogmatic belief behind such denial that the Goddess would be unhappy if women were included in the worshiping procession as it is assumed that the women on account of their biological functions would disturb the serenity and piousness of the high hills. (Nautiyal, Annpurna 2005) However after many decades women asserted their wish and rights to take active part and from 1987 onwards women are being allowed for the same. These kinds of persisting biases in the society obstruct the women's empowerment. There is a need to pay serious attention to the fact that if the women in subsistence economies are the major suppliers of food, fuel, and water for their families, and yet their access to productive resources is declining, then more people will suffer from hunger, malnutrition, illness, and loss of productivity. Investing in women is the fastest way to increase food security, controlling the population growth and relieving pressures on the environment. After having dealt with the symptoms, roots and consequences of gender biases, it is necessary to present the strategies to address the same. Traditionally, there are three strategies- the strategies of rap groups, the strategies of egalitarian ethics and liberation ethics to address such problems but they have their own merits and demerits which would be analyzed in the following section of the present paper.

PART THREE

As suggested in the beginning of this paper, that addressing gender biases is one of prominent mechanism to achieve the goals of women empowerment. As stated earlier that the complex socio-cultural-religious traditions are responsible for creating gender biases. The persisting biases are continuously playing the roles of helping and supporting the discrimination against women in the day to day functioning. The discrimination on the basis of sex as well as the gender biases is reflected in the various spheres whether it is letting the females to come into the world, providing nutrition, opportunities for education, interaction and choosing the life the way they want to live. In fact the socio-cultural and religious traditions create a kind of bias, which hampers the capacity of judging between wrong and right. Thus, the discrimination against women dominates not only the routine actions but their right of interaction and sharing is also harassed. On account of denial to provide equal opportunities to grow and enhance their potential and capacities a kind of injustice is being done to them. In addition, their rights to live, think, plan and act accordingly are not allowed; rather they are made captive to the decisions taken by the male members of the family.

In such scenario, even the strong mechanism of education, health, and economic empowerment may not be able to address the biases in the holistic manner and until the very attitude of the men and women are changed the society would continue to suffer from the biases. If an honest and serious attempt is to be made for providing the women their dues the gender bias thinking would have to be changed. However the approach and attitude of a biased society can neither change overnight nor is it easy to change it. To bring a change in the mentality is a time taking process which also requires the moral strategies. In view of this the first and foremost need is to formulate moral strategies for interaction and exposures, providing equal status and liberating not only women but also the entire biased community. It is also worth mentioning here that across the world efforts are being made to address this particular issue and there are three models (Freeman, Jo 1972) of moral strategies to initiate the attempts to address gender biases: the RAP group initiatives, the moral goal presented by egalitarian ethics and the third women liberation ethics emerged from movement in the field. All the three models of moral strategies have their merits and demerits therefore before the proposed strategy to address gender biases is analyzed, it is necessary to examine the existing three models with a purpose to utilize their merits and leave the demerits aside.

The theoretical formulation of RAP group is focused on two main purposes. The first objective is traditional and the other is the unique one-raising consciousness through sharing. The traditional role is the simple process of bringing women together in a situation of structured interaction. The hypothesis behind it was the acceptance of the fact that people can be kept in a state of subordination as long as they are kept divided from each other and relating more with those in a similar position will give them the strength. Women have been largely deprived of a means of structured interaction and have been kept isolated in their individual homes. The RAP groups initiated to create an artificial structured platform specifically for altering the participants' perceptions and conceptions of themselves and society. The other objective was aimed at 'the consciousness rising through sharing of the personal feelings' (Freeman, Jo 1972). The public sharing of the personal experiences led to realization that what was thought to be individual is in fact a common reality, what was thought to be personal problem has a complex socio-cultural and religious background as the cause. The exercises undertaken by the women-folk taught them to see how social structures and attitudes have molded them from birth and limited their opportunities. The male dominating thinking is ascertained up to the extent women have been suppressed in the society and it was also meant to judge how they have developed the prejudices against themselves as well as other women. Though the spirit of the RAP group was innovative, but when the attempt was made to deal with the biases through its application it faced some problems. The fundamental objectives of the particular effort were enlisted as - correcting the consciousness, resocialization and consciousnesses rising, all goals were achieved but the achievement was momentary. Since the effort made an absolute division between male and female and overlooked the fact that after the meeting points the women have to get back to their homes and share the already shared feeling with their male counterparts who are still in the clutches of gender bias thinking. Consequently, women had to face opposition at the domestic fronts. Due to non – participation of male folk in the ongoing structured interaction invited their opposition at the domestic levels and as a result, the participation of the women declined because for the women the first preference is always her home and family. On the basis of the above analysis, we can say that absolute division of male and female group cannot work to address the issue of the gender bias attitude, because since the society is constituted of men and women and by rectifying the perception of one group and leaving aside the other one can not address the problem in a holistic way. Though it is only effective mechanism to make the sufferers realize their sufferings and sharing the feelings of the group of sufferer gives the strength to raise the voice against injustice, still it was temporal one and could not be taken to be effective for a longer time.

All the formulations of moral strategies were meant to improve the conditions of women through getting her equal status and liberations from the prison of dogmatic biases against her. From this point of view, the strategies of egalitarian and liberation ethics are important and need to be analyzed. The egalitarian ethics presupposed that sexes are equal: therefore, sex roles must be equal without any discrimination. The history has proved that institutionalized differences inevitably mean inequality and determined roles because the particular sex (male in this sense) has reached to the levels of anarchism. The metaphysical analysis finds its roots in the division of labor as has been expressed "strongly differentiated sex roles were rooted in the ancient division of labor; their basis has been torn apart by modern technology." (Freeman, Jo 1972) Their justification was rooted in the subjection of women to reproductive cycle. But the need of hour is that the cramped little categories of personality and social function to which we assign people from birth must be broken and be opened so that all people can develop independently as an individual. The major problem regarding this moral model of addressing gender biases was that the increased similarity of the two groups increased not only options for individuals but also increased the diversity in the human race. Actually the need of the hour is to create a pattern where there is no division of men's work and women's work and the humanity also stops suffering a schizophrenic personality disorder of maintaining its masculine and feminine parts separately. No longer would marriage be an institution where two half of the people come together in hopes of making the whole. Thus instead of putting the two groups into the one, it is required to protect the identity of men and women and provide them equal opportunities to realize their full potential.

The liberation ethics model to address gender biases is a further step to egalitarian ethics. It incorporates the fundamental spirit of objectives set to be achieved by egalitarian ethics and tries to meet the challenges on the theoretical grounds. Pointing out shortcomings of egalitarian ethical models, the liberation ethics say that the attempt of egalitarian ethics is not enough to achieve the objective. The change of the limits of the roles is not the only requirements, but their content also needs to be modified. The strategy of liberation ethics looks at the kind of lives currently being led by men as well as women and suggests that both are deplorable. At the same track, social institutions which oppress women as women and oppress people as people can be altered to make a more human existence for all. The liberation ethics has expressed in its spirit that men and women both should be treated as independent persons and not subordinate to any one. What is meant to be an independent person has been explained by Peter Kemp in the following words; "I am a person from the moment I discover myself and understand myself as a will to life and at the same time I discover others as a condition for explaining and expanding the capacities of my own life. A person is then a self conscious physical being who lives by receiving something and giving something to other self conscious physical being." (Peter, Kemp 2005) The concept of person as narrated by Peter Camp may be the guiding instruction in determining the status of women as independent individuals. If women are given the opportunities to expand and explain their own capacities as an individual and establishing the positive relations to the other components of their surrounding they would definitely get a balanced approach, concern and development. But it is ironical that despite women's sacrifices most of their belonging and capacities for the family and society are ignored as these are considered compulsory duties of the women. In order to remove the condition of compulsion the definition of Peter Camp needs to incorporate the autonomy of will in exchange process even if it is for her sake. Maeve Cooke has rightly stated this; "The concept of person implies an autonomous will. Hence autonomy suppose on the one hand a separation from others by which an individual has specific personality and on the other hand an association with others by which others recognize ones self as autonomous. However, self-autonomy can be interpreted in terms of capacities such as responsibilities, accountability, independence etc. Ethics interpretation of human well being presupposes the individual's capacity to develop and pursue one's own conceptions of Good". (Maeve Cooke 2005)

To recapitulate the essence of the three models of moral strategies to address gender bias, it can be said that the RAP group strategy advocated the absolute separation of men and women and overlooked their coordination and co-operation which is needed for a healthy and balance society. It is necessary to include both the counterparts while proposing any strategies. In the same way the egalitarian ethics advocated absolute equalization without acknowledging the concern for each other. Both the strategies actually opted for extremist ways. The liberation ethics proposes equality and exchange of interest and consequently has been referential and relative. Thus there could be a balance between serving her own interest as well as concern and care for others. For the purpose of incorporating the merits of all the three models of moral strategies to address the gender bias attitude it can be said that the liberation ethics model of moral strategies seems to be most appropriate and balanced approach to address this piquant issue of gender biases.

Conclusion

It has been almost more than thirty years of intensive efforts of addressing the issue of women empowerment yet the efforts are not yielding desired result in terms of reducing the gender bias approach both in strategy formulation as well as implementation. Obtaining liberation from being the second category citizen and getting the equal status is the main objectives of all the movements for the empowerment of women. However, it is also ironical that the theoretical and practical efforts have not been complementary to each. Whenever the opportunities to encourage women has been provided either through education or through financial support in the planning at government level or NGO, the efforts have been more focused on addressing the implications and results of gender bias that make a women weak, but these programmes do not have long-term strategies to address the roots of the problems. Since the roots of problem i.e. women's secondary position lies in the gender bias attitude it should be address through the moral strategies. In addition, the strategies of RAP group or egalitarian ethics will serve the objective of addressing the problem only partially. To address the problem of gender bias in totality there is a need to take dual steps: firstly addressing the attitude modification and inculcating the aspiration to get liberation from the binding category and getting equal status through the interactions. But the participation of likeminded males would be necessary as they would be instrumental in rectifying the wrong perceptions of other male members in the society. After looking at the merits and demerits of the three models of moral strategies it can be proposed that the liberation ethics may fulfill the objective if taken in the proper perspective. It is necessary that all the steps should be taken for a holistic treatment of problems. Both at the level of formulation of theoretical- moral strategies as well as the level of implementation of the programmes a very sensitive kind of ethical approach is needed and the objectives could be fulfilled by the strategy of liberation ethics. The following narration that provides a complete picture of ethical concerns for the purpose of addressing the issue of gender bias can work as a guiding principal. "An ethics of care commences with the picturization of moral universe where the attitude of care, co-operation and relationship replaces conflicts, crisis and collision. In the so called moral universe the abstract principles of individual autonomy, rights and duties, justice, rules and laws are devalued and the feminine qualities of friendship and mothering are esteemed." (Waren Karen J 1997)

References

www.legal-explanations.com/definitions/**gender**-bias.htm

Singh Abha;(2005) Towards Women Empowerment, Indian Philosophical Quarterly, Vol. XXXII No 1-2 January-April

Das, Arpana Dhar: (2005) Eco-feminism, Indian Philosophical Quarterly, Vol. XXXII No 1-2 January-April

Sen, Amartya: (1998) Individual Freedom, in Times of India 16th October.

Jodi L. Jacobson: (2007) Gender Bias Causes Poverty, Population Growth World Watch Mission report.

Nautiyal, Annpurna; (2005) Roots of Gender Disparity in Garhwal Himalaya: From Eco-Social Disparity to Eco-Political Activism, in JSAWS Vol.10, No.2 March, 26.

Freeman, Jo: (1972) The Women Liberation Movement: Its Origin, Structures and Ideas Pub. In 'Family, Marriage and the Struggles of the Sex, ed. By Hans Peter Dreitzd, the Macmillan & Co.

Peter, Kemp; (2005) From Ethics to Bio-ethics in Questioning Ethics ed. Richard Kearney and Mark Dooley, Routledge London and New York.

Maeve Cooke; (2005) Questioning Autonomy in Questioning Ethics ed. Richard Kearney and Mark Dooley, Routledge London and New York.

Waren Karen J: (1997) The Power and Premises of Ecological – feminism in Theories of Ethics and Practice; ed. By Hugh Lafollette, Blackwell philosophy.

13

Culture of Peace through Strengthening Women's and Minority's Rights

Pushpa Motiyani

"Mahatma Gandhi taught that if all men and women, whatever the difference between them cling to the truth with respect for the unique dignity of every human being, a new world order - a civilization of love can be achieved. And today we hear him still pleading with the world. "Conquer hate by love, untruth by truth, violence by suffering." (**Pope John Paul II Times of India February 3,1986)**

We live today in possibly the most exciting age of human; an age of rapid and profound transformation. These transformations which are taking place in political, economic, social, scientific and environmental spheres have on the one hand posed many challenges, but on the other, there is a tremendous increase in knowledge, resources and global awareness, to tackle them successfully. Today, the biggest challenge is to eradicate poverty in the developing countries and to make available to the masses the benefits of the increase in knowledge in science, technology and other spheres. In the last forty years, the benefits of the development have not reached to the poor of the developing countries adequately. The main reason behind this, is the fact that, there are political, social and economic inequalities between and within nations. Ultimately, these inequalities lead to serious power differences, as a result of which the benefits of development are reaped only by ruling classes. Unless we solve the developmental problems of these depressed masses of the developing countries, we cannot think of a just world order, based on human rights and peace.

Development is a process (means) to achieve the objective (goal) of human rights and peace. In western countries, the continuous economic development has not created the conditions for peace, while in the communist countries the basic material needs of the people have been satisfied but the condition of human rights have not improved. After the political independence most of the developing countries, have followed the path of planned development. But, this development has only been able to strengthen the traditional inequalities. The main reason behind this, is the fact, that the development has always been centered around the economic sphere, while human needs, social and ecological factors have been neglected. Therefore, Culture of peace includes a fight against poverty, discrimination, exploitation and injustice. Thus, violence and war are also the product of social tensions as disparities and denial of justice. Here Peace is not merely the absence of violence and war. It is a dynamic process involving individuals and communities in dialogue and action to achieve a state of calm and blissfulness. Culture of Peace is a set of values, traditions and modes of behaviour based on respect of life, end to violence and the promotion of social change through Education, dialogue and conflict resolution. Unless these root causes are removed, peace will remain a distant dream. Culture of Peace means justice, freedom, equity, tolerance and sharing. (Mathur, J. S)

So Culture of Peace and Non-violence require the basic fundamentals of humans such as equality, liberation and justice, which is possible through the culture of human rights. A culture of human rights is growing throughout the world a well civilized world society, where human rights are not against anyone but for everyone. A society possessing human rights gives due respect, status and dignity to all others which will lead world civilization towards coexistence and international brotherhood. Under such circumstances, no man is tortured, no man is abused and no child is denied his or her dignity. (Federico Mayor, 1996) In such societies where human rights are preserved and this atmosphere prevails it will lead to a non-violent society.

The concept of human rights is a concept of world order. It is a proposal for structuring the world so that every individual's human worth is protected (Derica, Petrica M. 1981). Human rights are necessary to protect human dignity and values so that by developing its potential he/she can contribute to the betterment of the society. From the dawn of civilization, the rights of human beings were derived from the law of nature, religion and human experience. These have determined the declaration of the human rights. Human rights' existence was important due to its resistance to' tyranny and oppression. The enlightened awareness of deprivation of rights of people in various places of the world at different times, made the human rights movements to get its momentum, particularly it was familiar in the Western Civilization. While all popular revolutions secured human rights through bloodshed, violence and war but India has contributed to traditions of non-violence, of peace-making and culture of peace throughout history. In a life dedicated to peace and social justice, Mohandas Gandhi, perhaps the greatest figure in the history of non-violence, preached these values through constructive programmes. Today the need of the hour is to establish the Culture of Peace to remove structural violence from the society. This can only be achieved through absence of exploitation, communal riots, gender and all kinds of discrimination etc. Perhaps Gandhiji was the first person who introduced non-violence and its techniques and adopted "welfare of all" while fighting for the genuine rights of people in South Africa and India. (Shah Mahendra 1989)

For Gandhi the individual human being was the supreme consideration. He says, *"No society can possibly be built on a denial of individual freedom. It is contrary to the very nature of man. Just as man will not grow horns or a tail. So, he will not exist as man, if he has no mind of his own. In reality even those who do not believe in the' liberty of the individual don't believe in their own."* In Gandhian perspective, the individual is the prime concern and the state exists for the development of the individual. He remarked, 'I would feel that if we succeed in including the character of the individual the society will take care of itself. I would be quite willing to trust the organization of society to individual so developed. "Such a refined individual becomes the maker of his/her own destiny. Actually we are the makers of our destiny. We can't mend or mar the present and on that the future will depend." One can find the following distinctive basic features of Gandhi's approach to human rights:

- Human being is the supreme consideration.
- Rights are inherent in human beings, irrespective of religion, race, colour, nationality, etc.
- Peace is the prerequisite for all.
- Meeting the basic needs of all is embedded in Sarvodaya.
- Welfare of all.

In Gandhiji's views, duty is the prime thing, which would be the precursor of right, therefore, 'rights are earned.' He says "Rights accrue automatically to him who duly performs his duties. In fact the right to perform one's duties is the only right that is worth living for and dying for. It covers all legitimate rights. All the rest is grab under one guise or another and contains in it seeds of Ahimsa." (Collected Works of Mahatma Gandhi). Therefore, Gandhi drew a dear difference between rights and duties, as he stated, "There is a distinction between right and duty. The exercise of right depends on one's sense of duty. It is my duty to follow dharma. I do not think only of my own importance. It is of no consequence to me. I think in terms of the nation. I do what I consider my duty". Gandhiji declared that "rights are duty bound action, which will definitely bring enjoyment of rights; for that, selfless action is a must. Therefore, action is duty, fruit is right".

The entire realm of Gandhian thought and action was to liberate man from the clutches of domination, exploitation and violence. He disciplined himself using non-violence as a means to solve human problems. Thus, he became a fighter for human rights with his unique and powerful non-violent weapon of Satyagraha. As Gandhiji stated, "But to him who observes truth and non-violence comes prestige, and prestige brings rights. And people who obtain rights as a result of performance of duty exercise them for the service of the society never for themselves". (Collected Works of Mahatma Gandhi) In South Africa he fought not only for the rights of the Indians, but also to reform the community. For instance the Indians were indifferent to public hygiene. Gandhiji not only exhorted them to keep their houses and surroundings clean but also helped them to organize -themselves for that purpose.

In South Africa, for the first time Gandhiji revolted against colour, a discrimination practiced by the South African Government on Indian settlers. Gandhiji resorted to awareness - building programmes among the Indian settlers so as to acquaint them with the technique of non-violent resistance. Gandhi could achieve the legitimate rights of Indian settlers by retaining their Franchise and succeeded in the non-violent fight against 'Black Act' taxes and other imposed restrictions on the

Indian settlers. Therefore, the Gandhian philosophy which is based on Indian culture is more concerned with duties than with rights. We may not be unduly concerned with our own rights, but we must respect the sacred rights of other human beings with meticulous care. It is the very basic of Gandhian philosophy that we respect the personality of the fellow human beings. The experience of non-violent mass struggle led by Gandhiji in South Africa was quite useful for him to liberate the Indian people from the British colonial rule in India. Therefore, Gandhiji before launching a non-violent freedom struggle, had to practice and train' the people in nonviolent action inculcating non-violent 'values and virtues.

Gandhiji strove hard to secure the rights of minorities In India, for that he asked the majority to safeguard the minorities and expected that "the strongest should act as a shield to the weakest." (Collected Works of Mahatma Gandhi) Under his leadership the well-knit non-violent Indian Peace movement against communalism tried to unite all minorities to the national cause. In particular he identified the Harijan, tribals and women's upliftment. To maintain inter-religious harmony, Gandhiji gave equal status and importance to Muslims, Christians, Parsis, Sikhs and Hindus'. His mission to Naokhali for the Hindu-Muslim unity was remarkable and exhibited his art of peace making particularly for rights of minorities. Gandhiji urged and educated the Indian masses, the necessity of removing all disabilities imposed on depressed classes. Similarly Gandhiji evolved constructive programmes mainly for the upliftment of weaker sections. Particularly he included communal harmony and removal of untouchability. The great Mahatma Gandhi argued that women were able to save the world. He looked on women as the incarnation of ahimsa (Utne Birgit Brock, 1984) women have a different upbringing from men; they are a more peaceful sex and more capable than men of solving conflicts in a non-violent manner. He warned women against imitating men, becoming like men. He felt that women can run the race but she will not rise to the heights she is capable of by mimicking man (Gandhi, Mahatma 1940) .This sentence resembles a feminist adage of recent origin; the woman who strives to be equal to a man lacks ambition. Gandhi said that he had learnt the techniques of non-violence and civil disobedience from women, mainly from the British suffragettes.

Gandhi was convinced that women should take the lead in the civil disobedience or Satyagraha movement in India. He said, "l would love to find that my future would contain a vast preponderance of women over men. If the fight came, I should then face it with greater confidence than if men predominated. I would dread the latter's violence. Women would be my guarantee against such an outbreak" (Gandhi, Mahatma, 1939) . Actually, more than 60 percent of the participants in the Salt March were women. And out of the 30,000 people arrested in connection with the March, 17,000 were women (Thoman. P. 1964,) Recent opinion polls in the western world seem to show that women have a different attitude from men to the military, to the arms race and to the question of which means to use in order to reach the end of a peaceful and disarmed world. Throughout his life, Gandhiji maintained and worked for the equality of woman with man. He believed in woman's ability, strength, will and character to stand on her own and to work with man. Gandhiji, had awakened the women folk, and made them to fight for their rights and freedom. He brought them into political arena from their home and made them to take active part in the Indian freedom struggle. He held that 'the salvation of India depended upon the sacrifice and enlightment of women.' He advocated that contribution of women in non-violent warfare be more than that of men. As he told at time of the salt Satyagraha (1930) that "in this non-violent movement their contribution should be much greater than men's contribution". (Collected Works of Mahatma Gandhi)

To call women the weaker sex is a libel: it is men's injustice to women. If strength means brute strength, then indeed women are less brute then men. If strength means moral power, then women are immeasurably superior to men. Without her man can not be complete and if non-violence is the law of our being, the future is with women. Women suffer many indignities such as child-marriage, ban on widow-remarriage, lack of education, dowry and the evil customs of Devadasi among the Hindus and Purdah among the Muslims. Gandhiji was aware of this and advised women to be men's companions and comrades, in common service. Gandhiji said, "If you want to play your part in world affairs, you must refuse to deck yourselves for pleasing men and to revolt against the concept of women are born to be men's plaything." According to Gandhiji "the wife, is not the husband's bond-slave but his companion and his help-mate and an equal partner in all his joys and sorrows and as free as the husband to choose her own path." (Bose N. K) Therefore, he advocated equality of sexes and stressed that if women are the ones who have the potential for saving the world, they ought to be given a prominent position in society. But as we know, this is not the case and throughout the world women are rather second class citizens, are oppressed and exploited. Frequently quoted United Nations statistics state that women are doing two-thirds of the work in the world (paid and unpaid), receive ten per cent of the salaries and own one per cent of property.

Gandhi was of the opinion that even in the context of marriage women should guard against serving, as mere tools of enjoyment for their men. He urged women to refuse to play along by dressing to please man, which could only confirm their subordinate status in the world. (Motiyani, Pushpa, 1998) In the address to women in Ceylon 1927 Gandhi said: "What is it that makes woman deck herself more than man? I am told by feminine friends that she does so for pleasing men. Well, I tell you, if you want to play your part in the world's affairs, you must refuse to deck yourself for pleasing man. If I was born a woman I would rise in rebellion against the pretension on the part of man that woman is born to be his plaything."(Gandhi,

Mahatma 1927) Gandhi's vision of the role of women in Indian society, and his stand on specific social reform issues, were remarkable. Gandhiji voiced opposition against child marriages. For him, marriage was not a license for physical union but a sacrament, imposing discipline on the partners. An ideal marriage according to him, is one which leads to spiritual union through physical union. In Gandhiji's firm opinion wives should not be looked upon as dolls or objects of indulgence but should be treated as honoured comrades in common 'services'. He opposed the evil custom of child-marriage. He tried to mobilize public opinion against such evils. Gandhiji also voiced against dowry system as it was a cruel custom which turned young girls as an object to be bought and sold. He made fervent appeal to unmarried young men and women - especially educated young men and women not to accept this cruel custom. Gandhiji protested against prostitution which he termed as moral leprosy but not against the prostitutes, who were to be pitied and helped to regain their virtues. Gandhiji also did not believe in the utility of purdah, and a woman with the purdah was not necessarily purer than a woman without it. To him the system was "'vicious, brutal and barbarous."

So far as remedial measures for eradicating these evils are concerned, Gandhiji advice to the women was to rely on themselves and their inner strength than on men. He exhorted women to be completely fearless and maintained that education should aim at character-building, fostering moral values and enabling them to walk freely with men. His advice to the educated women was to conserve the best traditions of Indian culture and reject that which is based on discrimination of genders. Once addressing women college students, he observed that, "Your parents do not send you to school to become dolls; on the contrary, you are expected to become sisters of Mercy." Gandhiji believed that the secret of achieving world peace is equally in the hands or women and men. To attain peace in every walk of life a cumulative effort of both men and women backed by nonviolence, justice and equality is essential.

In conclusion we can say that Gandhiji can be called a peace-maker because he worked earnestly for social justice. Also he gave importance to fulfilling the basic human rights which are the components of peace. Therefore, in today's world, if we want to establish a civilization of peace and nonviolence, there is an urgent need to give more importance to attainment of human rights of women, and weaker sections. Then only justice will be attained in the society which will abolish violence, discrimination, injustice towards women and the weaker sections and will lead the world towards a culture of peace.

References

Mathur, J. S. "Peace, Non-violence and World order - Gandhian Perspective" Vohara Pub., Allahabad - p. 104.

Federico Mayor, (1996)Director General - UNESCO, International Symposium on "Culture of Peace", 12-14 June, Proceedings, p. 22.

Derica Petrica M. (1981) - "Human Rights and International Law", Dept. of State Bulletin, Vol. 81, p. 23.

Shah Mahendra (1989) - " Human Rights, Peace and Development - In the Context of-Developing Countries", Unpublished Ph.D. Thesis, Gujarat Vidyapith, Ahmedbad. p. 76.

Collected Works of Mahatma Gandhi - Vol. 50, 69.

C. W.M.G., Vol. 69, p. 208.

C.W.M.G., Vol. 69, p. 52.

Kaka Saheb Kalelkar 'In Horizons of - Ed. L. M. Singhvi - p. 41.

Birgit Brock Utne (1984) "The Relationship of Feminism to Peace and Peace Education", Bulletin of Peace Proposal, Vol. 15, No.2, 1984, p. 149.s

Gandhi Mahatma (1940) " What is women's Role", Harijan, February 24.

Gandhi Mahatma (1939) "Swaraj through Women", Harijan, December 2,

Thoman. P. (1964,) "Indian Women through the Ages", Asia Publishing House,

C.W.M.G., Vol. 43, p. 219.

Bose N. K., Selection from Gandhi - p. 242.

Motiyani Pushpa (1998) "Mahila Vikas Ki Nai Dhishayen", Kamavati Publication, Ahmedabad. p. 98.

Gandhi, Mahatma (1927) "Women and Ornaments", Young India, December 8.

[illegible]

14

Empowerment of Women Through Political Participation

Anil Dutta Mishra

A.S. Altekar as rightly remarked “the degree of freedom given to women to move about in society and to take part in its public gives a good idea of the nature of its administration and enables us to know how far it had realized the difficult truth that women too have a contribution of their own to make to its development and progress” (Altekar, A.S. 1962). In fact if we wish to cure the traditional disease of Indian society, family and individual; if equality, freedom and justice is our goal and if future generations are to be nurtured in harmony, our social consciousness is to be restructured in a manner which may be free from masculine arrogance and social prejudices.

Despite their vast numerical strength, women occupy a marginalised position in Indian society due to several socio-economic constraints. Social evils like dowry deaths, polygamy, child-marriage, female infanticide, forced prostitution and crime against women have not been uprooted from our country. This has inhibited the effective participation of women in the political processes and institutional structures of democracy. According to the Document on Women's Development (1985), women's role in political process has virtually remained unchanged, despite the rapid growth of their informal political activities. A broad-based political participation of women has been severely limited due to various traditional factors such as caste, religion, feudal attitudes and family status. As a result, women have been left on the periphery of political life. Of late, steps have been taken to improve women's representation and the policy of reservation for women has been incorporated in the 73rd and 74th Amendments. Reservation of seats for women in the Panchayati Raj Institutions (PRIs) and municipal bodies will provide them with an opportunity to ventilate their grievances and to take active part in the formal political arena which deals with social and economic problems.

The system of Panchayati Raj, which was initiated mainly for people's participation in political and economic processes some how has not been successful in ensuring women's participation. The champions of the Panchayati Raj system desired that rural women should not only become the beneficiaries of development, but more importantly the contributors to it. The Balwantrai Mehta Committee was particular that women should find representation in the rural political institutions and recommended that two women should be co-opted in Panchayat Samiti. As a result of this recommendation, a few states did make provision for women's representation. But the system of nomination or co-option meant sheer patronage of the dominant political or social groups and the women who got nominated had practically no information on Panchayats nor any experience in working for women. Women's representation on these bodies came to be symbolized by 'tokenism' and not by a meaningful association. Therefore, some states gave up nomination or co-option and resorted to reservation as the only way of ensuring women's participation in the PRIs. But in the recent years, special efforts are being made to ensure women's representation in the PRIs in the wake of the 73rd Constitutional Amendment Act which reserves one-third of the seats for women in PRIs. The participation of women in PRIs is considered essential not only for ensuring their political participation in the democratic process but also for realising the developmental goals for women.

Participation and Empowerment: Women's Perspective

People's participation is a necessary pre-condition for the successful implementation of any plan programme. This is based on the assumption that the process of people's development is not likely to strike very deep roots unless the target groups themselves become part of it. Participation is a means of reducing power differences and is, therefore, contributory to equalization and social justice. Participation in public life has many facets. It includes activities which have strong bearing on group and the community, the power to effectively influence elected representatives, decision-making process as well as policies and actually alter existing situations wherever they are found to be clearly disadvantageous. While women should be positioned in large number at crucial levels for significant and effective exercise of power, they need to be equipped with suitable means to shoulder these -responsibilities. Otherwise their representation would end up as mere tokenism. (Country Report, Fourth World Conference on Women, Beijing, 1955) Political participation manifests itself in actual participation in those voluntary activities by which members of a society share in the selection of rulers and, directly or indirectly, in the formulation of public policy. It also includes such activities as voting, seeking information, contributing financially, discussing and proselytizing, attending meetings, communicating with representatives, enrolment in a party, canvassing and registering voters, speech writing and speech making, campaigning and competing for public and party office. (Vir, Dharam and Mahajan, Kamlesh, 1969).

Participation of women in politics involves: *(i)* women as voter; *(ii)* women as member of political parties, trade unions/ pressure groups; *(iii)* women as elected members of Parliament, State Assemblies and various bodies of local self-government and taking part in decision-making, planning, implementation and evaluation; *(iv)* women as members of women's organization and their association with voluntary organisations and NGOs. The concept of political participation of women is broader than the one covering women's participation only in the electoral and administration processes. It includes the gamut of voluntary activities with a bearing on the political processes, including voting, support of political groups, communication with legislator, dissemination of political views and opinions among the electorate, and other related activities. However, political participation can be considered to include an involvement in any form of organized activity that effects, or seeks to affect, these power relationships. It refers broadly also to "activities by those not formally empowered to make decision, these activities being mainly intended to influence the attitudes and behaviour of those who have powers for decision making". (Gupta, Sunita and Gupta, Mukta, 1966) In fact, protests and demonstrations against those in power also form part of political participation. Women's participation has covered a range of activities including movements, protest and support meetings on all issues connected with labour, dowry, rape, domestic violence, pressurize, food adulteration and deforestation, as also movements for the promotion of peace. (Gupta, Sunita and Gupta, Mukta, 1966)

Explaining the importance of participation in politics, Milbrath and Goel argue that the citizens must at least participate in the choice of their public officials in order to keep public action responsive to the wishes and desires of the people.

(Milbrath, L.W., and *Goel,* M.L. 1977) In fact "participation in politics and in public debate helps to build a better and nobler character in the people... People would be better human beings if they, so participated". Similarly McClosky said participation benefits the participants as well as the larger community. According to N.D. Palmer, participation helps the individual to be effective and it associates him or her with the political system. The higher the rate and levels, the more varied the forms of participation, the healthier is the democratic system. (Palmer, N.D. 1976)

Participation enables women by giving them a sense of their own dignity and value. For women participation has three roles: educative, integrative and empowering. Women constitute half the society and belong to all classes and all sections. So, the women's empowerment is not the question of one section only. It is ultimately the question of the entire society. It is an integral part of the entire social phenomenon. Human society cannot move forward without stirring half of its body, the women. Thus, it is in the social and national interest to draw womenfolk into the social and political process. Today women are connected directly or indirectly to the operation of society at every level, and at the same time occupy the aggregate position of outsiders. No one can deny today the fact that for women's empowerment, participation at every level and in every field is essential.

The political space belongs to all citizens; politics is everyone's business and affects the lives of each of us... the more women are associated, in numbers corresponding to their percentage of the population, in the political decision making process, in parties, in elected bodies, in government and in international bodies, the more they can be associated with this process as protagonists and more they can change the modalities and outcomes of politics. Only then will the concept of democracy find concrete and tangible expression because democracy and the participation of women go hand in hand and promote each other mutually. (Inter-Parliamentary Union (IPU), *Reports and Documents* 1991)

Twentieth century has brought a great change in the life of women all over the world, influencing their attitudes, values, inspirations, ways of feeling, standards of behaviour and acting for effective participation in all walks of life. Women's quest for equality with men has become a global phenomenon. It is particularly relevant in the societies which have deep roots of patriarchy and subjugation of women. Gender division is found in all walks of life and which influences family, division of labour, class structure and nation states. As now, women are also involved in politics, developmental programmes, movements etc. therefore they are challenging the patriarchy. They are now coming out of their insulated enclosures and social spaces expressing their equality with men, freedom and dignity. They are resisting control of their sexuality by men. Caste, class and gender-based oppression of women are being opposed in several quarters in Indian society. Women's rights in land and property in actual life are being acknowledged as an instrument of their empowerment. The 73rd constitutional amendment has initiated a process of empowerment of women in India in general and the women of countryside in particular, which is the need of the hour. Although women are participating in ever greater numbers in politics and public life all over the world, but they still remain largely outside the realms of power and decision making in government. The gap between men and women's participation in political life have narrowed somewhat but it still remains huge, as figures about women as head of governments, holders of ministerial positions and member of parliaments indicate towards the poor representation of the women. ((Marilee Karl, 1955) In fact, women's participation in elections depends on the mobilization of the political parties, general awareness among the community of the importance of voting and the overall political culture. No serious efforts have been made to mobilise women as a political constituency by any political party, women are often projected as not being interested in and un-informed about political matters. Women are also not perceived as an organised interest or pressure group, so their needs are not taken into consideration. (Inter-Parliamentary Union (IPU), *Reports and Documents* 1991)

It is difficult, nonetheless, to generalise about the links between any single factor and political behaviour. They vary and are influenced by factors such as the social status of women, their economic position, cultural norms and above all, the regional outlook towards women's participation in public affairs. (Inter-Parliamentary Union (IPU), *Reports and Documents* 1991) The number of women contestants in parliamentary elections has not increased over years. Political parties are still reluctant to field women candidates. The high cost of election campaigning is a deterrent to women candidates. (Inter-Parliamentary Union (IPU), *Reports and Documents* 1991) In spite of these facts, woman in decision making and leadership roles at the grass-roots, regional and national level is a major change factor. (Inter-Parliamentary Union (IPU), *Reports and Documents* 1991) The key instruments of the strategy for women's development both as beneficiaries and as participants is, therefore *grass-root level* organizations of women for learning and productive activity, which would help: *(i)* to draw them into the mainstreams of development; *(ii)* promote self-reliance and collective action; *(iii)* strengthen their participation and voice in the development process; *(iv)* assist them to achieve economic viability as well as knowledge for their personal growth; *(v)* provide forums to enable women especially from the poorer sections to participate freely and fully in decisions that affect their lives and that of the community; *(vi)* enable them to acquire full access to development resources and services; and *(vii)* enable them to function as instruments of social change. (Gaur, K.D. 1996)

The process of empowerment is multi-dimensional and it enables women to realize their full destiny and powers in all spheres of life. Women's empowerment begins with consciousness-perceptions about herself and her rights, her capabilities and her potentials, awareness of how gender and socio-cultural and political forces affect her. Political empowerment, economic development and social upliftment of are necessary and desirable for the women to fight myriad forms of patriarchal domination, and discrimination at every stage. In fact, women's empowerment is central to the achievement of the triple goals of equality, development and social justice. And for that political participation is needed. In a democratic system, women's participation may be viewed at two levels, *(i)* awareness and assertion of women's political rights and *(ii)* acquisition and exercise of power.

Improving the political status of women in India is an integral aspect of the overall problem of socio-economic change and development. Do women politicians have different concerns or behave differently from men in politics and their participation make a difference to political issues and the way politics is carried out? Drude Dhalerup, who has carried out extensive research on women in politics, says: "Don't expect us to make much difference as long as we are only a few women in politics. It takes a critical mass of women to make a fundamental change in politics". (Dahlerup, Drude 1996) When significant numbers of women are in politics, as in the Nordic countries where women hold a relatively high percentage of elective positions in government, studies show that they do make a difference. As Dahlerup has opined that women politicians are just as powerless when it comes to the global economic changes as are the male politicians. But the many women in politics in the Scandinavian countries have to some extent changed people's attitude towards women as leaders, have changed the political discourse somewhat, have placed women's issues on the agenda, and have to some extent changed the political culture. (Marilee Karl, 1955) It is argued that if women in good number enter the corridors of power they will be able to take up women's issues within state structures and also effect changes in the party and local bodies. They will have access to state resources which can support women's groups and provide services to them. Their positions and actions can legitimize the women's cause in the eyes of the people and parties.

Women Participation in Indian Politics

The active participation of women in the freedom struggle developed an increasing sense of awareness to organize and lead the cause of their liberation from oppression and subordination simultaneously. After independence, a large number of legal and socio-economic measures have been taken to elevate the status of women. Women too, have become politically conscious as they have started participating in national and state politics. Independence of India opened the doors for the women of the country to find their due place in society and partake in the political, social and administrative life of the country. The advent of democracy in India brought forth the spectacle of women moving up along in the corridors of political power, which has brought them new opportunities both as voter and candidates. They entered the two houses of the Indian parliament in their own way and some of them made a mark therein. (Bhall, Shanta, 1995) Voting is the basic activity by which the citizen gets assimilated in the political process. Women's participation in formal elections is to a great extent dependent on the mobilization efforts of the political parties, general awareness among the community and the overall political culture. It is common experience that the percentage of non-voters is usually higher among women than men. But the recent studies indicate that the sex differences in political participation are diminishing. (Baxter, S. and Lansing, 1980). The study by Usha Mehta undertaken to examine the voting trend of man and women of the General Elections in India from 1952 to 1977 shows that the gender gap is diminishing in the voting. As can be assessed by examining the following table: (Chaudhuri, Senghamitra Sen, 1955)

Voting Turnout among men and women from 1952-1977 (Mehta Usha 1978)

	Voted		
Year	*Men (%)*	*Women (%)*	*Difference (%)*
1952	55.00	31.1	17.9
1957	56.00	39.6	14.4
1962	62.1	46.6	15.5
1967	66.7	55.5	11.2
1971	69.7	60.0	9.71
1977	65.62	54.91	10.71

However some other studies on political participation have exhibited that there is still a gender gap in the level of political information and perception regarding implications of various political issues (e.g. the right to franchise both quantitatively and qualitatively). The committee on the status of women has attributed this to the lack of interest shown by political parties in improving the political knowledge of women. (Chaudhuri, Senghamitra Sen, 1955) It is generally held that in spite of the growing equality between men and women in society, political participation is taken as more natural to men than to women. It is assumed that women voters vote as the male members of the family desire and as such no separate and special effort is usually made to mobilize them as participants in the voting act. (Chaudhuri, Senghamitra Sen, 1955)

But despite the problems the women are increasingly participating in the political process, as indicated in the following table by the shrinking gap of per cent of actual voters by sex. In 1962 the gap was more than 15 per cent. This declined steadily over different elections. In 1980, the gap was little over six per cent, but in 1984, it again went up to about 10 per cent. The number of women contestants to the Lok Sabha rose steadily between 1962 and 1980, but number of successful female candidates progressively declined till 1997 (from 33 in 1962 to 19 in 1977). But in elections of 1980 and 1984 the number of successful female candidates again increased to 28 in 1980 and 42 in 1984. However, women members still constitute less than 10 per cent of the total Lok Sabha seats. The picture is not better in the states as well . (Gupta, Sunita, and Gupta, Mukta, 1996)

Women Contestants for Lok Sabha from 1952-1989

Year	*Total No. of seats*	*No. of Women contestants*	*Percentage*
1952	487	43	8.8
1937	494	45	9.1
1962	491	69	14.0
1967	515	67	13.0
1971	518	85	16.4
1977	542	71	11.07
1980	542	142	26.2
1984	542	173	32.3
1989	543	189	34.8

These increasing figures are indicative of the fact that after independence more and more political consciousness and desire for greater political clout has grown among Indian women. However, this increasing participation of women is insignificant when we view this fact in the light of male participation. The participation of male members far exceeds the participation of women. The table given below testifies this generalization.

Women Contestants and Elected in General Elections from 1952-1996

Year	*Contestants*		*Elected*	
	Total	*Women*	*Total*	*Women*
1952	1974	43 (2.3)	489	14 (2.3)
1957	1519	45 (3.0)	494	27 (2.5)
1962	1938	69 (3.5)	494	33 (6.7)
1967	2369	67 (2.8)	520	30 (5.8)
1971	2784	85 (3.1)	518	21 (4.1)
1977	4371	71 (1.6)	542	18 (3.3)
1980		142	542	28 (5.1)
1984		142	542	43 (7.9)
1989		189	543	28 (5.1)
1996	13353	599 (4.4)	543	39 (7.1)

However, when we look at the number of women candidates actually elected to Lok Sabha in the various general Elections, we find their percentage increasing upto the 1962 elections and then it started declining. This indicates that the presence of women at the highest political levels coexists with a generally low rate of overall participation in the political life of the country. The table gives the number of women M.Ps and their representation. The Eighth Lok Sabha had the maximum and the Sixth Lok Sabha had the minimum representation of women members. (Bhall, Shanta, 1995)

As far as women's membership in the upper house as against the male member is concerned, the number of women in the upper house reached an all time high in 1977. In 1977, the number of women M.Ps was 25 (10.2%) of the total membership of Rajya Sabha except in 1957 and 1962, the percentage of women's representation in Rajya Sabha remained higher than that in the Lok Sabha. It must, however, be noted that most women in the rural as well as urban areas are still not fully participating in the political field and decision making processes of the nation. It does not mean that the status of women in India has not improved after Independence and that there is no social consciousness at all towards social reality. When one reflects upon the presence of women representatives in the corridors of power, one can not ignore the fact that we had a woman Prime Minister who had Olympian position in her nation's political system.

Number of Women Members in Lok Sabha

Lok Sabha Elections	*Year*	*Total No. of Seats*	*No. of Women Members*	*Percentage*
1st Lok Sabha	1952	499	22	4.4
2nd Lok Sabha	1957	500	27	5.4
3rd Lok Sabha	1962	503	34	6.7
4th Lok Sabha	1967	523	31	5.9
5th Lok Sabha	1971	521	22	4.2
6th Lok Sabha	1977	544	20	3.4
7th Lok Sabha	1980	544	28	5.5
8th Lok Sabha	1984	545	45	8.9
9th Lok Sabha	1989	543	28	5.1

Obstacles in Women's Participation

The participation of women is influenced by inter-related factors like the social status of women, their economic position, the cultural norms, and above all the regional outlook towards women's participation in the society. Access to significant decision-making position in the political parties continues to elude women. Women in the political world face peculiar problems which are totally unknown to their male counterparts. These inhibit their performance in the legislative and party work not only in India but also in the so-called emancipated societies of the developed countries. A variety of reasons account for women's diminished role in the political arena. These include tradition, physiology, lack of vertical mobility, concern for home and family, psychology and lack of patronage, particularly, from senior women politicians. In other words, political participation of women is severely limited due to a nexus of traditional factors like domination of Indian politics by patriarchal forces and the consideration of caste, class, religion, feudal and family status etc., all of these are parochial and favour men more than women. Consequently, women are still left on the periphery of the political process, and their political participation remains basically confined to elections. At the same time, there are several other socio-economic constraints which marginalize the women. Due to this the number of women in leadership positions at the local, village, district and national level is still not commensurate with their numbers in society. A woman in public life at the different level is as much part of the Indian Society as the woman who is confined to her home and family. Styles of functioning of such women in the three tier system of Panchayati Raj, or State Assemblies or Parliament are bound to be shaped by the cultural mosaic which is studded with the prescriptive and descriptive elements, codes of conduct, role models, political goals, values and ideals in transitions.

The United Nations Divisions for the Advancement of Women (DAW) has identified a number of obstacles to women's participation in politics which prevent them from reaching parliamentary and ministerial positions:

- the relatively short historical tradition of women's political participation and lack of experience in campaigning, public debate, exposure to media;
- prevailing negative attitudes towards women's participation in public life, lack of confidence and support for female candidates and politicians on the part of the electorate, including women;

- the difficulty women experience in combining a political career with the traditional women's role in the family and often in society;
- economic dependency or lack of financial means; insufficient education in general and political education in particular;
- Women's reluctance or diffidence to participate in politics, particularly at a high level. (Marilee, Karl 1955)

Mechanism to Increase Women's Participation

Empowerment is not a technocratic goal-it is a wholesale Political commitment. Achieving it requires a long term process in which all cultural, social, political and economic norms undergo fundamental change. It also requires an entirely new way of thinking-in which the stereotyping of women and men no longer limits their choices, but gives way to a new philosophy that regards all people as essential agents of change that views development as a process of enlarging the choice of both sexes, just not one. Stages of emancipation of women, in any given country, lie in the mind of man and in the attitudes of their leadership. And these two factors have mostly favoured women in India. Besides this training is one of the most important mechanisms for improving women's participation in politics particularly for increasing women's access to the higher levels in national decision making bodies. Whilst training can be directed to improving women's skills in specific areas, particularly in management, in addition gender sensitivity training can be directed to both men and women to build awareness of the concrete and attitudinal barriers to women's participation, advancement and empowerment. Nehru held the view that women "must" be trained to participate "in every department of human activity" and play an active part in all professions and spheres.

In some countries quotas have been successfully used to increase women's participation in the leadership of political parties and in party lists for public election. For instance, the Norwegian Labour Party stipulates that at least 40 percent of all candidates for election must be women. The Danish Social Democratic party has a similar provision for municipal and country elections. According to the Norwegian Labour Party's Secretariat, "Quotas for Women is the most efficient strategy we ever used to increase women's political representation". (Marilee, Karl 1955) The constitutions or legislation of only few countries provide for quotas for women in parliament, including those of Angola, the former USSR and Nepal. In addition, the 1991, electoral law of Argentina establishes a compulsory 30 percent quota for women candidates for all effective posts. Related to the quota system is the mechanism of reserved seats: Bangladesh, Egypt, Nepal, Pakistan and the United Republic of Tanzania are the countries that have or have had in the past a certain number of seats in their national parliaments reserved for women. (Marilee, Karl 1955)

The under representation of women in political decision making bodies is the key reason for the backwardness of Indian women. To ensure the women's participation the 73rd and 74th Amendments of the constitution mandated 1/3 reservation of 'seats for women in all local level elected bodies. Similarly there is a need of reservation of seats in parliament and State Assemblies also. Reservation of seats in the legislative bodies for women will alter the very character of the legislative body and will compel the political parties to change their strategies and tactics and induce them to give women their due. If the women enter these bodies in larger number, inhibitions that result from their minority position in these institutions may disappear fast and give them greater freedom to articulate their views. A system of reservation may also increase the women legislators' sense of responsibility and concern for the problems affecting women as well as ensure the presence of a body of spokesmen of the women's cause in the representative bodies of the states. Such a system would also help to increase the degree of political modernization of women both in the electorate and within the parties. (Chaudhuri, Senghamitra Sen, 1955)

Political education and awareness building is intended to promote women's representation in the electoral process; to establish and lobby for a women's agenda; and to sensitize both women and men to women's issues and the role of women in politics. For promoting awareness it is necessary to organize from time to time a series of seminars, workshops and conferences all across India to involve women in political debate and present their views. These workshops will reach a wide cross section of women. An expert group meeting on Equality in Political Participation and Decision-making organized by DAW made the following recommendations to women's status in political parties:

- as an interim measures, substantial targets, such as quotas or similar forms of positive action to be ensured

- 'women's candidacy for office and participation in political posts should be applied;

- training programmes should be developed to increase the political and management skills of women in politics, both as candidates and as elected or appointed officials, especially making use of the experience of other women who have achieved public office;

- women's sections of parties should be evaluated and strengthened to enable them to influence party policy and promote female candidacy;

- information on potential women candidates should be compiled, maintained on a systematic basis and made available when candidacy or appointments are considered;

- parties should be encouraged to examine the criteria used to select persons for political functions to ensure that the varieties of experience possessed by women are taken into account in selection;

- training activities should be developed to sensitize party members to the needs and potentials of female members;

- as an interim measure where the electoral system might make it useful, parties should undertake special measures to provide funding for women candidates for office. (Chaudhuri, Senghamitra Sen, 1955)

Other important mechanism includes networking, participation in the campaigns of other politicians, lobbying, and membership in the same clubs, professional and academic associations. (Marilee, Karl 1955) The corrective mechanisms are to be viewed holistically and not as isolated piecemeal actions. Only then the women will be at par with men in all fields.

Conclusion

Manu's dictum that she should do nothing independently even in her own house. In childhood subject to her father, in youth to her husband, and when her husband is dead to her sons, she should never enjoy independence have proved wrong. Now women have come out of their isolation, got themselves educated, stormed male bastions in jobs and services and also have the backing of constitutional safeguards and social legislation. Women need to make themselves politically visible and important in order to change the direction of development, empowerment and gender justice. Unless deep-rooted changes in power relations between men and women are brought about things are not going to change. Rays of hope are becoming brighter and radical changes in and through participation in social political process, will be instrumental to women' empowerment. Women's empowerment is essential and desirable for societal development. A society attempting to develop without the full participation of women is like bird trying to fly with only one wing. It is therefore necessary to let the women realise their immense potential for social change, to rise up and excel as the builders of nation. At the same time women must take upon themselves the task of participating in political and economic affairs with commitment and a sense of challenge and men must also readily accept women in their new roles.

Notes and References

Altekar, A.S., (1962) *Thee Position of Women* in *Hindu Civilisation,* Varanasi, Motilal Banarsidass, p. 9.

Country Report, (1995) Fourth World Conference on Women, Beijing, 1955, New Delhi, Government of India, , p. 66.

Vir, Dharam and Mahajan, Kamlesh, (1969), "Contemporary Indian Women," *Collected Works,* Vol. 4, *Politics, Awareness and Women's Movements,* Delhi, New Academic Publishers. p. 121.

Gupta, Sunita and Gupta, Mukta, (eds.) (1966) *Role of* Women in *the Twenty-first Century,* Delhi, Anmol Publications. p.63.

Milbrath, L.W., and *Goel,* M.L. (1977) *Political Participation: How and Wiry, Do People Get Involved* in *Politics?,* Chicago, Rand McNally. p.2.

Palmer, N.D. (1976) *Elections and Political Development in India,* New Delhi, Vikas. pp. 59-61.

Inter-Parliamentary Union (IPU), (1992) Women and Political Power Survey Carried Out Among the ISO National Parliaments as of 31 October, *Reports and Documents,* No. 19, p. 1.

Karl, Marilee, (1955)*Women and Empowerment, Participation and Decision Making,* London and New Jersey, Zed Books Ltd. p. 59.

Gaur, K.D. (1996) "Women and Governmental Programmes", in Dharam Vir and Kamlesh Mahajan (eds.), *Contemporary Indian Women, Collected Works,* Vol. 4, New Delhi, Academic Publishers. p. 177.

Dahlerup, Drude, (1996) "From a Small to a Large Majority: Women in Scandinavian Politics", quoted in Virginia Willis, "Public

Life: Women make a difference", paper for the *Expert Group Meeting on the Role of Women in Public Life, DAW,* Vienna, p. 10.

Bhall, Shanta, (1995) *Women Parliamentarians of India,* Udaipur, Shiva Publishers and Distributors, p. 44.

Baxter, S. and Lansing, M. (1980) *Women and Politics: The invisible Majority,* Ann Arbor, University of Michigan Press, pp. 24-27; S. Welch "Women as Political Animals: A Test of Some Explanations from Male-Female Political Participation Differences," *American Journal of Political Science;* 21 November, 1977, pp. 711-33; K. Anderson "Working Women and Political Participation 1952-1972", *American Journal of Political Science,* 19 (August) 1975, pp. 433-53.

Chaudhuri, Senghamitra Sen, (1955) *Women and Politics: West Bengal a Case Study,* "Calcutta, Minerva Associates, p. 24.

Usha Mehta (1978) Reports of Election Commission of India in "Indian Women and their Participation in Politics", *Social Change,* Vol. 8, No.3, September, p. 32.

Gupta, Sunita, and Gupta, Mukta, eds. (1996) *Role of Women in the Twenty first Century,* Delhi, Anmol Publications, pp. 46-47.

15

Uttarakhand: Problems of a New State

B.C. Upreti

In multi-structured societies various types of movements leading to the demand for autonomy is a common and continuous phenomenon. Such demand largely emanate due to the majority-minority conflicts, rise of ethnicity, threat to cultural identity, discriminatory policies followed by the government leading to women development and marginalization of a community or a region. The people of such community or region feel that they are being discriminated in terms of socio-economic development and political representation. These feelings encourage them to launch a movement based on their separate ethnic or regional identity or both. The nature and extent of the movement and the extent of realization of the aspirations of the people depend on, leadership of the region and their capacity to bargain or influence the central leadership. A federal political structure has been viewed a viable media in the multi-structured societies to satisfy strong autonomy tendencies by way of granting them statehood. This, however, does not mean to argue that federalism can or does provide answer to all sort of ethno-regional demands and issues. It is actually a political issue and realization of regional demands in terms of granting the status of a state autonomy depends on many political considerations. Nevertheless, it can be said that a federal political structure is a flexible system and can provide room for the settlement of the ethnic or the regional issues.

Uttarakhand being a distinct geographical unit from the rest of its parent state Uttar Pradesh, having a separate socio-cultural and economic identity and being a backward region had legitimate claims for a separate statehood. It is not therefore a debatable issue whether or not Uttarakhand should have been given the status of a separate state. Also it is a fact that all such distinct geographical regions with their distinct cultural identity were granted statehood earlier, as and when demands were raised for such a status. It is also a fact that not only the Uttar Pradesh state was a very vast state, but Uttarakhand region faced numerous administrative and policy-planning complexities due to the different geographical nature of the region.

Idea of Himalayan States

Why has the need for a separate Himalayan state occurred? What is its relevance? There are significant issues and need some explanations. It may be pointed out here at the outset that the concept of a hilly or Himalayan state is a post independence phenomenon. At the time of independence of India Assam was the only hill state. In October 1947 Jammu & Kashmir emerged as the second hilly state after the merger of Kashmir state with the Union of India. The other hill areas were parts of the one or the other larger state of India.

It was realized after a certain period of time that in terms of development and planning the hill areas were lagging behind in comparison to the developmental activities taking place in the plains areas of such states. One important reason behind this difference was the different geographic and socio-economic context of the hilly areas. It needed a different approach and different focus. These regions gradually began to realize that they were lagging behind in the process of development. It was also a matter of discontent that these regions because of their isolated geographical situation were being discriminated by the state governments. Therefore, in order to give a special consideration to the hilly regions they were given a distinct status. They were considered as a specific development unit. In 1961 Nagaland became the third hilly state followed by Himanchal Pradesh in 1971. Other hilly states which came up subsequently are Meghalaya, Manipur, Tripura, Sikkim, Arunachal Pradesh, Mizoram and Uttarakhand.

S.No.	*Year*	*State*	*Capital*	*Area in Sq. Km.*	*Population*
1.	Before 1947	Assam	Dispur	78438	2655528
2.	1947	Jammu & Kashmir	Srinagar	222236	10143700
3.	1966	Nagaland	Kohima	16579	1990036
4.	1971	Himanchal Pradesh	Shimla	55673	6077900
5.	1972	Meghalaya	Shillong	22429	2318222
6.	1972	Manipur	Imphal	22183	2166788
7.	1972	Tripura	Agartalla	10486	3199203
8.	1975	Sikkim	Gangtok	7096	540851
9.	1987	Arunachal Pradesh		83743	1097968
10.	1987	Mizoram	Izol	21081	888573
11.	2000	Uttarakhand	Deheradun	53484	8489349

These Himalayan states have many common aspects. Their developmental problems and challenges are similar, although these states are at different stages of development. Is it possible for these states to share their common needs, problems and experiences together and envisage a common perspective goals and policies is an important issue and needs a serious thinking.

Birth of a New State

The idea of a separate state of Uttarakhand constituting the Kumoun and Garhwal regions of Uttar Pradesh first came up in 1938 during the Shrinagar Conference of the Indian National Congress Conference. But this idea remained on papers and it was not much discussed afterwards. During the 1950s P.C.Joshi raised the issue of separate state of Uttarakhand. Again it remained confined to the intellectual and political discussions. It was, however, argued that the process of modernization and development was marginalizing the people of Uttarakhand. The development process initiated in the region had ignored local needs and aspirations and it was benefiting the outsiders, who could make use of the resources of the hills with the growth of infra structural facilities there. In July 1979, Uttarakhand Kranti Dal (UKD) was launched. Its single objective was to attain the separate statehood to Uttarakhand. Thus, it was a party that owes its origin to the demand of a separate state of Uttarakhand. The party initially had lots of enthusiasm and tried to launch a systematic movement for a separate state. Its objective was dual: to mobilize local support and to pressurize the state and the central governments to attain its objective. There is no doubt that the UKD did lot of groundwork but it could not do much at the electoral front. The factionalism within the party gave birth to a number of splinter groups that weakened the movement and the party as well. It is for these reasons that the UKD could not mobilize people beyond a limit. Other political and non-political groups had to join it. It is interesting to note that Kumoun and Garhwal have been giving political leadership of national structure since the days of Uttar Pradesh but they remained silent on the issue of a separate state for the hills of Kumoun and Garhwal.. After independence a number of leaders belonging to this region occupied high positions in the party and the government. But on the question of a separate state for the hills they maintained a silence. The major political parties began to take interest on the issue of separate state of Uttarakhand since 1991. The movement for Uttarakhand received momentum after 1994. The UKD became a major force behind the movement. But once the Uttarakhand state came into existence in 2000, UKD went into the background. Initially it was decided that instead of going for fresh elections as assembly would be constituted out of the members of the legislative assembly of Uttar Pradesh elected from the areas that constituted Uttarakhand state. The BJP being the largest party got opportunity to form the first government of Uttarakhand state. However, the party had to go for a change of Chief Minister before elections for the state assembly took place. But that also did not help the party in the elections that took place. The Congress party secured majority and a senior political leader Narain Dutt Tiwari was given the challenging task to head the government. The recent elections indicate that the incumbency factor is important in the politics of the state. Now it is the BJP, which has been given the mandate to form government under the leadership of Gen. B.C. Khanduri.

Uttaranchal to Uttarakhand

The movement for a separate state in the hill areas of Uttar Pradesh began with the demand that a separate state of Uttarakhand be constituted out of Kumoun and Garhwal regions. The regional party that emerged in the wake of the movement for a separate state also named itself as Uttarakhand Kranti Dal. But the BJP Government at the centre giving the reason that the BJP do not believe in divisions named it as Uttaranchal in place of Uttarakhand. However people believed that as the naming of the state as Uttarakhand could have given an edge to Uttarakhand Kranti Dal therefore the BJP, while looking for its own prospects of coming to power in the newly constituted state and to deny any advantage to other parties preferred Uttaranchal in place of Uttarakhand as the name of the new state. This led to the politics of name and provoked the anger and unhappiness among the Uttarakhand Kranti Dal and many groups and individuals in the state. Towards the completion of the tenure of the Congress government the issues of naming of the state again came up and the Congress mooted a proposal to rename the state as Uttarakhand and the central government readily accepted the proposal. The Congress government of Uttarakhand took the credit of once again renaming the state from Uttaranchal to Uttarakhnad just when the elections were round the corner. Why this issue did not come up earlier is a moot question. The clear massage is that the Congress government was trying to appease those people who were not happy with the naming of the state as Uttaranchal and thus emerged the politics of naming and renaming the state among the two main political parties of the state. While Congress' gimmick of renaming Uttaranchal as Uttarakhand was aimed towards taking credit for respecting and exploiting people's sentiments associated with Uttarakhand however it could not help it to improve its performance in assembly elections. The anti incumbency factor assured that the politics of name is not going to work in its favour and the BJP formed the government. These developments have identified BJP with Uttaranchal and the Congress Party with Uttarakhand. While the Uttarakhand Kranti Dal and sections of the people of Uttaranchal who had advocated Uttarakhand initially as name for the state are totally isolated in this respect. How BJP as a party in power in the state would look at this issue is still to be seen.

The Issue of State Capital

Another issue that flared up with the granting of statehood to the hill areas was that of the capital of the newly created state. A bureaucratic decision was taken to declare Dehradun as the temporary capital of the state. Dehradun being a well-connected and well-developed city was advantageous for a state capital in many ways as far as the establishment is concerned. But Dehradun being situated in a plains area is quite far off from the main hill areas. Those who were associated with the movement for statehood believed that the state capital should be some where in the remote hill areas for providing the benefits of the statehood to the inhabitants. Secondly, it was also thought that the area should be located some where in the middle of the two regions: Kumoun and Garhwal, so that both the regions could be represented equally. It is true that the establishment of a new capital will require huge funds. But then it can be said that such an approach followed by the UKD and others was based on the ground realities. Despite the establishment of a commission to look in to the merits and demerits this issue is still not resolved and is likely to come up again and again as people in many parts are voicing their anger through observing fasts, dharans, rallies etc. The commission has submitted its report but the governments have yet to act on its report.

Delimitation of Boundaries

Yet another complex issue, which was associated with the emergence of the new state, was the delimitation of its boundaries. A controversy was raised regarding the inclusion of Udham Singh Nagar and Haridwar in the new state. The Akali Dal of Punjab pleaded that Udham Singh Nagar would not be made a part of Uttarakhand. Perhaps the party thought that the Sikhs residing in Udham Singh Nagar may not receive proper treatment in the new state. It was indeed a wrong notion because there was hardly any sort of adverse perception about the settlement of Sikhs in Udham Singh Nagar and the rest of the Tarai. Moreover, they were a minority when this region was a part of Uttar Pradesh but they never received any ill treatment from the state government. After a long debate that the two cities were given to Uttarakhand. It may be pointed out here that the plains area of Tarai though a small land area is very important for the state. It can be said that it is a lifeline for the economy of the hills. It not only holds most fertile land of the state but also provides opportunities for industrialization, particularly heavy and agro based industries. Hence, depriving

Uttarakhand of these regions would have been a great economic loss to the state. The Tarai belt has larger employment opportunities for the people.

Local Issues, Problems and Politics

There had been certain local issues that always vitiated the social and political environment of the hills of Uttarakhand since the earliest times. The issue of Kumoun vis-à-vis Garhwal had deep roots. There had been historical animosities between the two regions of Uttarakhand. When the demand for a separate hill state came up doubts were raised regarding the understanding between Kumoun and Garhwal. After acquiring the statehood this issue has not came up and it is a positive development. But the people know it that it is a fiery issue and needs a broad based approach for socio-economic development for its natural liquidation. The state leadership needs to follow a cautious approach in this regard and no politics should be played over it.

The Brahmin-Thakur caste politics has also been a serious issue in Uttarakhand. It was expected that the caste politics would take a back seat after the formation of Uttarakhand state. But it is clear that the caste politics has aggravated in place of its liquidation. The leadership conflicts are surfaced along the caste lines. It can be said that the caste rivalries have vitiated political atmosphere in the state. It has indeed weakened the state leadership and reduced the prospects of development in the region.

The issue of hills vis-à-vis plains is also not less significant. It was indeed a compulsion for the Uttarakhand state to incorporate within it some of the plains areas. But it is a well known fact that the plains areas have been a bone of contention for the hill areas for many reasons. How to resolve this dichotomy is a big question. The geography of the two regions cannot be undone. The hills will remain hills and the plains as plains. There are socio-cultural differences and different levels of development and conflict over resources in the plains areas among the different sets of migrants. There is larger concentration of population in the plains. Therefore they have more representatives in the state legislative assembly. The hill people have been demanding delimitation of constituencies on the basis of area instead of population. Thus the hill-vis-à-vis plains have become a strange phenomenon. On the one hand the state has to struggle to keep plains areas with it and on the other hand there is a conflict of hills vis-à-vis plains. The leadership needs to tackle this issue in a manner so that the sentiments of the people are not hurt. The places like Haridwar not only have religious importance but they also provide opportunities for employment. The cities like Haldwani, Deharadun, and Haridwar are important business centers and meet the requirements of the hill people in various ways. Therefore, plains areas have immense significance for Uttarakhand. Any move to de link these areas can be considered as conspiracy against the state. There are problems too since these areas are densely populated therefore it may create problems for the rest of the region. The question of hill vis-à-vis plain people is important in whole of the Tarai region of Uttarakhand. But as said earlier, this region has economic significance and the state authorities have to be careful about its claims over these regions in future as well. This discussion gives some idea about the fact that the beginning of the Uttarakhand state has not been as smooth as it was thought to be. Some of these issues are still alive and may again come up in future.

Socio – Economic Issues

But the real challenge for the Uttarakhand state is its socio-economic development. It is not that Uttarakhand is a resource less state and despite lot of depletion Uttarakhand is still rich in forest resources. These resources can be developed for multiplier benefits. Horticulture can be developed further and development of medicinal herbs can be beneficial. Uttarakhand has vast scope for religious and recreational tourism and the development of tourism and trekking particularly in the lesser-known areas of the state needs proper infra-structural development. There is also scope for animal husbandry sheep and Goat keeping in the upper and lower Himalayan region in a planned and scientific manner which can be beneficial in a number of ways. Uttarakhand is also rich in river water-resources. These river water resources can be developed for the generation of hydropower which can be used for earning revenue for the state. But if any of the future hydropower projects meets the same fate as the mega Tehri dam project then there is no use of having such resources. It is indeed unfortunate that for over 50 years we have not been able to fix up our long-term developmental approach. The point is that there are resources and potentials but the only need is to lay down clear-cut developmental priorities and policies. How long a state can survive on the special funds received from the central government? Ultimately, it has to develop its own resources. That is the real challenge before the Uttarakhand state today.

People have been migrating from Uttarakhand and settling down in the far flung cities of plains for a long time. Economic backwardness and the lack of employment opportunities of the region have been the primary reasons for migration of the people particularly the male migration. This process continues even today as even after the creation of the state the employment opportunities could not be created as per the necessity of the people of the hill areas of Uttarakhand. Though many of the migrants of Uttarakhand occupy very high positions in the government, education, science and technology, executive and other professions but except for some emotional feelings, they hardly have any role to play for their native state. It is a loss to the economy, institutions, society and culture of the state. No government can bring them back. It is a loss forever. But can this process be stopped now? This would require expansion of employment opportunities, establishment of scientific and research institutions, establishment of industries and so on. The government will have to expand the service sector and provide adequate infrastructure facilities for the growth of private and professional sectors. It may also be pointed out here that migration is a two way process in Uttarakhand. While people have been migrating to the plains in search of employment, there is also in- migration to this region from the plains. Particular the business and trading people have migrated to the big and small cities of Uttarakhand. Not only that the small scale industrialists, contractors, mine owners, etc. are also plains people. They have purchased land from the local people and have become permanent settlers. In fact, they dominate trade and industries in Uttarakhand. After a certain period of time the local business class may find it difficult to compete with the migrant business class. The local people may also find it difficult to get employment in private sector, industries and labour works. A situation may come up which the northeast is facing today. But we never try to learn from the history. The government of the day needs to follow a forward-looking approach in dealing with these issues so that the state does not face a movement like 'sons of the soil' of Assam. The local entrepreneurs have to be encouraged and out migration from the state have to be restrained so that the state does not face a gap in terms of resources and manpower, because these are two vital reasons for immigration.

The society in Uttarakhand, particularly, the rural society is undergoing a rapid change. With the development of means of transportation market has expanded to the farthest corners of the rural areas. All types of goods ranging from vegetables of plains, edibles to luxury items are available everywhere. Small markets have developed even in isolated villages. There is a demand for modern items in the villages. Even for grains and other edible items people are increasingly becoming dependent on market. They do not seem to be interested in agriculture and other traditional household works, as it is easy to purchase these from the market. Since one or two persons of majority of the families in Uttarakhand are employed outside and send money to them on a regular basis it is possible for them to purchase goods. The expansion of market economy has also brought a gradual change in the life style of the rural people. The traditional ways of celebrating festivals are changing. Similarly the marriage and such other occasions are also undergoing a change. Earlier such occasions were totally dependent on local means. But now there seems to be a lust for modernized celebrations. This has on the one hand increased dependence on market and affected the local economy on the other. Because of expansion of market people are no more interested in preserving their traditional means of economy. The rural economy of Uttarakhand is becoming outside based market economy. These trends are not encouraging, as this would largely increase external dependence of the region. If the present scenario of the rural Uttarakhand continues it may lead to economic stagnation. Therefore, a dynamic approach is needed to revitalize the rural economy with its maximum dependence on local resources and localized development opportunities.

Uttarakhand is passing through a complex situation. In order to envisage a development framework for the region the state leadership will have to understand the challenges coming up after the formation of the state, specific needs and problems, the nature and dynamics of socio-economic transformation taking place particularly in the rural areas and preservation of the material and human resources and its best possible utilization for the development of the state.

In the last paper of this volume "Uttarakhand: Problems of a New State' B.C. Upreti discusses about the problems of the newly created state of Uttarakhand. In the background of the paper he has given the emerging trends in all the Himalyan states to trace out the common aspects. He has highlighted that their developmental problems and challenges are similar, although these states are at different stages of development and raises the question whether it is possible for these states to share their common needs, problems and experiences together and envisage a common perspective goals and policies. This is an important issue and needs a louder thinking. He feels that the new state of Uttarakhand is passing through a complex situation. The causes of complex situation are the problems being confronted by the new state. In the beginning there was a controversy on the name of Uttarakhand and at present also the controversies like the issue of shifting the state capital to some remote hill area, delimitation of boundaries, local issues and politics, socio – economic issues are creating problems for the state. His suggestion is that in order to envisage a developmental framework for the region the state leadership will have to understand the challenges coming up after the formation of the state, specific needs and problems of the people of hill areas, the nature and dynamics of socio-economic transformation taking place particularly in the rural areas and preservation of the material and human resources and its best possible utilization for the development of the state.

Index

C

D

Y